THE WILD HISTORY OF THE AMERICAN WEST

WHAT MADE THE WILD WEST WILD

Wim Coleman and Pat Perrin

MyReportLinks.com Books

an imprint of

 Enslow Publishers, Inc.

Box 398, 40 Industrial Road
Berkeley Heights, NJ 07922
USA

MyReportLinks.com Books, an imprint of Enslow Publishers, Inc. MyReportLinks®
is a registered trademark of Enslow Publishers, Inc.

Library of Congress Cataloging-in-Publication Data

Coleman, Wim.
  What made the Wild West wild / Wim Coleman and Pat Perrin.
    p. cm. — (Wild history of the American West)
  Includes bibliographical references and index.
  ISBN 1-59845-016-6
  1. West (U.S.)—History—19th century—Juvenile literature. 2. West (U.S.)—Biography—Juvenile
literature. I. Perrin, Pat. II. Title. III. Series.
  F591.C65 2006
  978'.02—dc22

                              2005027979

Printed in the United States of America

10 9 8 7 6 5 4 3 2 1

To Our Readers:
Through the purchase of this book, you and your library gain access to the Report Links that specifically
back up this book.
The Publisher will provide access to the Report Links that back up this book and will keep these Report
Links up to date on **www.myreportlinks.com** for five years from the book's first publication date.
We have done our best to make sure all Internet addresses in this book were active and appropriate when
we went to press. However, the author and the Publisher have no control over, and assume no liability
for, the material available on those Internet sites or on other Web sites they may link to.
The usage of the MyReportLinks.com Books Web site is subject to the terms and conditions stated on the
Usage Policy Statement on **www.myreportlinks.com.**
A password may be required to access the Report Links that back up this book. The password is found
on the bottom of page 4 of this book.
Any comments or suggestions can be sent by e-mail to comments@myreportlinks.com or to the address
on the back cover.

Photo Credits: Commonwealth of Pennsylvania/Department of Environmental Protection, p. 43;
© Buffalo Bill Historical Center 2004, p. 93; © Corel Corporation, pp. 52, 54, 59; © Ibis
Communications, Inc., p. 105; © 1995 PhotoDisc, Inc., p. 28; © 1997 Boettcher/Trinklein Television,
Inc., p. 61; © 1997 University of Nebraska Press/U.S. Department of the Interior, p. 110; © 1999–2003
PBS Online/WGBH, p. 63; © *The Sacramento Bee,* p. 70; © 2000 Elizabeth Larson, p. 16; © 2001
Elizabeth Larson, p. 37; © 2001 Smithsonian Institution, p. 58; © 2001 THE WEST FILM PROJECT and
WETA, p. 11; © 2003–05, Legends of America.com, p. 48; © 2003 Pony Express National Museum,
p. 56; © 2003 Texas Ranger Hall of Fame and Museum, p. 83; Corbis American Destinations, p. 89;
CyberSoup.com, p. 13; Emily Zimmerman, p. 35; Enslow Publishers, Inc., pp. 5, 50; Library of Congress,
pp. 1, 3, 7 (dog and man panning for gold, Indian chief), 14, 19, 24, 26, 30, 40, 41, 45, 66, 72, 74, 76,
81, 87, 91, 94, 97, 98, 100, 103, 106, 108–109, 112; MyReportLinks.com Books, p. 4; Photos.com, pp. 6
(background), 7 (buffalo and wagon train), 68; Timothy Miller, University of Kansas, p. 86;
TheHistoryNet.com, p. 9; U.S. Bureau of Land Management, p. 78; U.S. Department of the Interior,
pp. 21, 32, 34, 64, 85; William Henry Jackson, p. 46, www.GhostTownGallery.com, p. 114.

Cover Photo: Library of Congress

Cover Description: Scene from a poster advertising Buffalo Bill's Wild West Show created by Courier
Lithograph Co. of Buffalo, N.Y. around 1899.

CONTENTS

MyReportLinks.com Books
Great Books, Great Links, Great for Research!

The Internet sites featured in this book can save you hours of research time. These Internet sites—we call them **"Report Links"**—are constantly changing, but we keep them up to date on our Web site.

When you see this "Approved Web Site" logo, you will know that we are directing you to a great Internet site that will help you with your research.

Give it a try! Type http://www.myreportlinks.com into your browser, click on the series title and enter the password, then click on the book title, and scroll down to the Report Links listed for this book.

The Report Links will bring you to great source documents, photographs, and illustrations. MyReportLinks.com Books save you time, feature Report Links that are kept up to date, and make report writing easier than ever! A complete listing of the Report Links can be found on pages 116–117 at the back of the book.

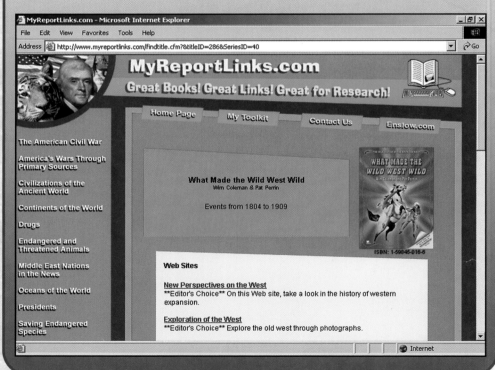

Please see "To Our Readers" on the copyright page for important information about this book, the MyReportLinks.com Web site, and the Report Links that back up this book.

Please enter WWW1077 if asked for a password.

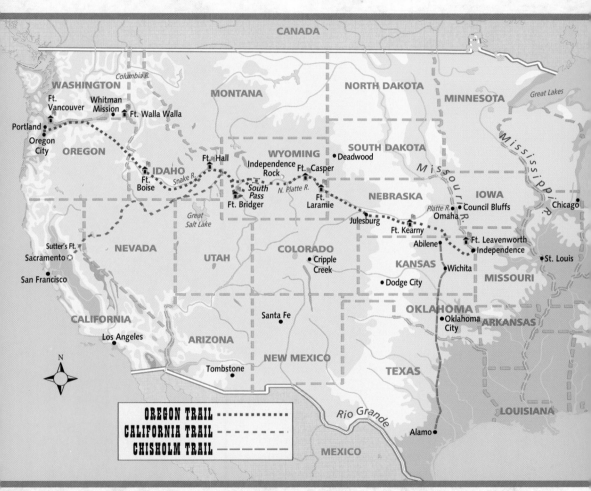

CANADA

WASHINGTON

Columbia R.

Ft.
Vancouver   Whitman
Mission   ● Ft. Walla Walla

Portland ●
Oregon
City ●   OREGON

MONTANA

NORTH DAKOTA

MINNESOTA

Great Lakes

Mississippi R.

SOUTH DAKOTA

● Deadwood

Ft. Hall   WYOMING   *Missouri R.*

Ft.
Boise   IDAHO   *Snake R.*   Independence
Rock   Ft. Casper

South
Pass   *N. Platte R.*   NEBRASKA   IOWA   Chicago ●

Ft. Bridger   Ft.
Laramie   *Platte R.* ● Council Bluffs
Omaha ●

Great
Salt Lake   Julesburg   Ft. Kearny

NEVADA   UTAH   COLORADO   Abilene   Ft. Leavenworth
Independence ●

Sutter's Ft.
Sacramento ⚬   KANSAS   Wichita ●   St. Louis ●

San Francisco   ● Cripple
Creek   MISSOURI

● Dodge City

CALIFORNIA   Santa Fe   OKLAHOMA   ARKANSAS

Los Angeles ●   ARIZONA   ● Oklahoma
City

N   NEW MEXICO   TEXAS

Tombstone ●   LOUISIANA

OREGON TRAIL · · · · · · · · ·
CALIFORNIA TRAIL – – – – –   *Rio Grande*
CHISHOLM TRAIL — — — —

MEXICO   Alamo ●

A map of well-known places and routes of the Wild West.

WILD WEST TIME LINE

▷ **1804**—President Thomas Jefferson sends Meriwether Lewis and William Clark on an expedition into the newly purchased Louisiana Territory. They return in 1806 reporting abundant beaver in the western mountains (in addition to other important information about the West).

▷ **1822**—The Rocky Mountain Fur Company advertises for young men to work with trapping teams in the Rocky Mountains. The trappers hold their final rendezvous in 1840.

▷ **1826**—Jedediah Smith leads the first group of Americans overland to California.

▷ **1836**—David Crockett, Jim Bowie, and many others die at the Battle of the Alamo.
—Texas declares its independence from Mexico.

▷ **1841**—The first wagon train of pioneers crosses the Rocky Mountains.

▷ **1846**—A treaty with Great Britain sets the northwest boundary with Canada where it is now.
—War with Mexico begins. When Mexico surrenders in 1848 the United States gains California and the Southwest.

▷ **1848**—Gold is discovered in California, at Sutter's Mill. By 1849, the "forty-niners" rush to California for gold.

▷ **1850**—Allan Pinkerton opens his Pinkerton's National Detective Agency, using the motto "We Never Sleep."

▷ **1852**—The first cattle drive from Texas to New York.

▷ **1858**—John Butterfield's Overland Mail Company begins stagecoach service between St. Louis and Los Angeles. In 1861, the completion of the Transcontinental Railroad brings cross-country stagecoach service to an end.

▷ **1860**—The Pony Express begins service in April. It closes down in November 1861, soon after the completion of a transcontinental telegraph line.
—Texas cowboys begin driving herds of cattle to markets in St. Louis and Chicago.

▷ **1861**—The American Civil War begins. In 1865, the Confederacy surrenders.

▷ **1866**—Jesse and Frank James lead an outlaw gang that commits bank and train robberies and murders.
—Belle Starr, who has known the James brothers and other outlaws since her teen years, begins her own outlaw career. She calls herself "The Bandit Queen."

▷ **1867**—The first cattle drive on the Chisholm Trail from Texas to Abilene, Kansas.

▷ **1869**—Ned Buntline's *Buffalo Bill, the King of the Border Men* runs as a series in *The New York Weekly.*
   —Hunters begin the destruction of the huge buffalo herds on the plains. Ten years later, the buffalo are nearly extinct.

▷ **1872**—The play *Buffalo Bill, the King of the Border Men* opens in New York City with an actor playing the lead. Later that year, Buffalo Bill (William F. Cody) and Texas Jack (J. B. Omohundro) play themselves in Buntline's *The Scouts of the Prairie.*

▷ **1873**—Buffalo Bill, Texas Jack, and Wild Bill (James Butler) Hickok play themselves in *The Scouts of the Plains.*

▷ **1875**—Wild Bill Hickok, now marshal in Deadwood, South Dakota, is shot in the back and killed.

▷ **1878**—Billy the Kid (William H. Bonney) leads an outlaw gang, rustling cattle. He has already killed several men.

▷ **1876**—The James Gang is broken up by lawmen. In 1879, the James brothers form a new gang and begin new robberies.

▷ **1880**—Lawman Pat Garrett kills Billy the Kid.

▷ **1881**—The last big cattle drive to Dodge City.

▷ **1882**—Jesse James is shot in the back and killed by a member of his gang.

▷ **1883**—Buffalo Bill Cody organizes "Buffalo Bill's Wild West Show."

▷ **1889**—Belle Starr, "The Bandit Queen," is shot in the back and killed.

▷ **1890**—The Dalton brothers form a gang and begin robbing gambling houses, trains, and banks.

▷ **1892**—Angry citizens gun down the Dalton gang.

▷ **1902**—Owen Wister's novel *The Virginian* is published. The novel and movie versions of it that follow present the cowboy as a noble figure.

▷ **1903**—With *The Great Train Robbery,* cowboy movies begin.

▷ **1905**—Tom Mix, movie-star cowboy, rides with the 101 Ranch performers in New York City's Madison Square Garden.

▷ **1909**—Butch Cassidy and the Sundance Kid are supposedly killed in Bolivia, bringing the era of western outlaw gangs to an end.

TELLING THE STORIES

"Wild Bill" Hickok, the folk hero, was lurking in the shadows, half hidden behind a gnarled oak tree. Suddenly, a strong light fell directly on Hickok. He whipped out his gun and, with his usual deadly aim, shattered the source of the light.[1] Everything went nearly dark.

The gnarled oak was only a painted tree, part of a set for a stage play in progress.

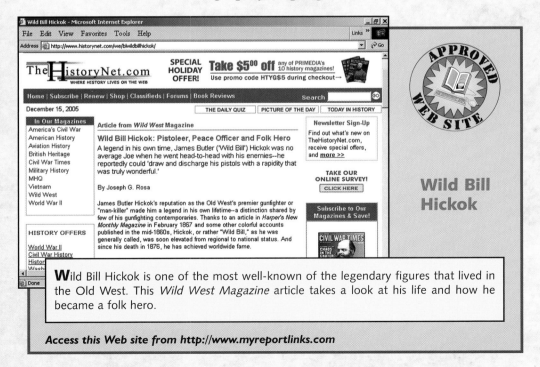

Wild Bill Hickok is one of the most well-known of the legendary figures that lived in the Old West. This *Wild West Magazine* article takes a look at his life and how he became a folk hero.

Access this Web site from http://www.myreportlinks.com

Wild Bill was in the play, but he did not like being in the spotlight. So he had blasted away the lighting equipment in the theater balcony. The rest of the men on stage, including "Buffalo Bill" Cody, went on with the show with the little light that was left.

Hickok and Cody were each playing themselves on stage in New York City. The play, *The Scouts of the Plains,* was a popular drama of the 1870s. It was just one of many stories that entertained eastern audiences with tales about the Wild West.

The Wild West on Page and Stage

Much of what we think of as the "Wild West" comes from stories that were told during the eighteenth and nineteenth centuries. Some of those western stories were factual and some were completely fictional. And many of those founded on facts were stretched quite a bit to make them more exciting.

Even while the West was being settled it was a source of entertainment. Dramatic events were quickly reported in newspapers, books, and on stage—very much the same way a hot story might be rushed into a book or a television movie today.

Author Mark Twain (Samuel Clemens) wrote for the Virginia City newspaper, *Territorial*

Enterprise. In an 1868 letter, Twain explained that the reporters sometimes made up stories that were published as news:

> To find a petrified man, or break a stranger's leg, or cave an imaginary mine, or discover some dead Indians in a Gold Hill tunnel, or massacre a family at Dutch Nick's, were feats and calamities that we never hesitated about devising when the public needed matters of thrilling interest for breakfast. The seemingly tranquil *Enterprise* office was a ghastly factory of slaughter, mutilation and general destruction in those days.[2]

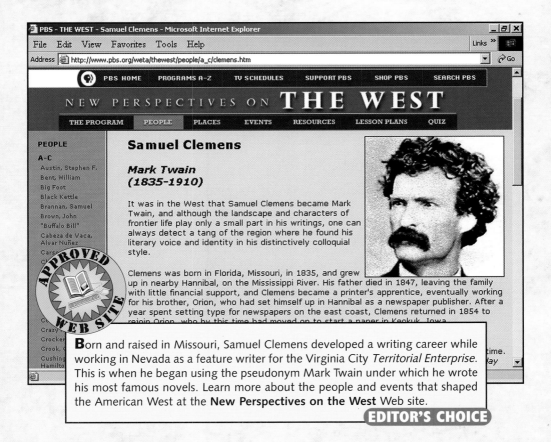

PBS – THE WEST – Samuel Clemens – Microsoft Internet Explorer

File   Edit   View   Favorites   Tools   Help   Links »

Address http://www.pbs.org/weta/thewest/people/a_c/clemens.htm   Go

PBS HOME   PROGRAMS A-Z   TV SCHEDULES   SUPPORT PBS   SHOP PBS   SEARCH PBS

NEW PERSPECTIVES ON **THE WEST**

THE PROGRAM   PEOPLE   PLACES   EVENTS   RESOURCES   LESSON PLANS   QUIZ

PEOPLE

A-C
Austin, Stephen F.
Bent, William
Big Foot
Black Kettle
Brannan, Samuel
Brown, John
"Buffalo Bill"
Cabeza de Vaca, Alvar Nuñez
Cars...
C...
Crazy...
Crocker...
Crook, ...
Cushing...
Hamilto...

Samuel Clemens

Mark Twain
(1835-1910)

It was in the West that Samuel Clemens became Mark Twain, and although the landscape and characters of frontier life play only a small part in his writings, one can always detect a tang of the region where he found his literary voice and identity in his distinctively colloquial style.

Clemens was born in Florida, Missouri, in 1835, and grew up in nearby Hannibal, on the Mississippi River. His father died in 1847, leaving the family with little financial support, and Clemens became a printer's apprentice, eventually working for his brother, Orion, who had set himself up in Hannibal as a newspaper publisher. After a year spent setting type for newspapers on the east coast, Clemens returned in 1854 to rejoin Orion, who by this time had moved on to start a paper in Keokuk, Iowa.

Born and raised in Missouri, Samuel Clemens developed a writing career while working in Nevada as a feature writer for the Virginia City *Territorial Enterprise*. This is when he began using the pseudonym Mark Twain under which he wrote his most famous novels. Learn more about the people and events that shaped the American West at the **New Perspectives on the West** Web site.

EDITOR'S CHOICE

APPROVED WEB SITE

Many western stories were about real people, and sometimes they were told by real men and women about themselves. The stories helped those people become legends in their own time.

American Legends

Legends are traditional stories that are based on real people or events. As they are told and retold, legends become more fantastic. Legendary heroes and villains might have done some of the things credited to them. But they most likely did not do them all.

For example, stories about powerful African-American railroad worker John Henry are thought to be based on a real person. According to a still popular song, "John Henry was a steel drivin' man" who died in a heroic effort to outwork a new machine—a steam drill. His legend lives on in story and song.

Daniel Boone was an expert hunter and trapper by the age of twelve. In 1769 he discovered the Cumberland Gap, a passage through the Appalachian Mountains. In 1774, Boone and his men started clearing the way for the Wilderness Road—making it easier for settlers and traders to travel west. According to stories about Boone, he once scared a bear out of a hollow tree by grabbing the bear's tail and yelling. And he once crossed a river by swinging on a grapevine.

David Crockett was another well-known frontiersman. He became a member of the United States Congress, and later died at the Battle of the Alamo. Crockett was known as the "coonskin congressman" because of the fur hat he wore. He became legendary as the great hunter and fighter "Davy" Crockett.

Stories about Davy Crockett grew quite outlandish. The tales say that he rode his pet alligator up the waters of Niagara Falls. He could ride the sun around the world and get off wherever he wanted to. Crockett also told some stories of his own. He claimed that one cold winter the earth stopped rotating. So he heated the oil from a small

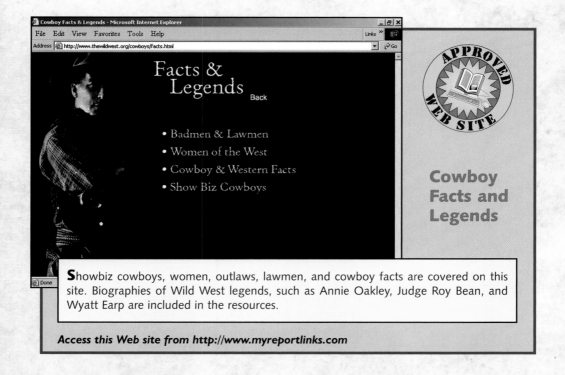

Cowboy Facts and Legends

Facts & Legends   Back

• Badmen & Lawmen
• Women of the West
• Cowboy & Western Facts
• Show Biz Cowboys

Showbiz cowboys, women, outlaws, lawmen, and cowboy facts are covered on this site. Biographies of Wild West legends, such as Annie Oakley, Judge Roy Bean, and Wyatt Earp are included in the resources.

Access this Web site from http://www.myreportlinks.com

▲ David "Davy" Crockett was a famous frontiersman and soldier of the Wild West. Many tales, both true and exaggerated, have been told about him.

bear, warmed the earth's axis, and got the earth turning again. In other words, Crockett was both a subject and a teller of tall tales.

Western Tall Tales

Tall tales are wildly exaggerated stories, usually meant to be funny. In a tall tale, the main character is much bigger than life. The main events could never happen in reality. The Wild West was full of tall tales, and we still enjoy many of them today.

Like Davy Crockett, Mike Fink made up his own tall tales. He was a trapper, scout, fighter, and often a mean-spirited practical joker. In the late 1700s, Fink was a keelboatman, carrying trade goods on the Ohio and other rivers. When they went upriver, keelboatmen had to pole their boats against the current. Keelboatmen had to be very strong, and according to this song, Fink claimed to be the strongest of them all:

> Oh, my name is Mike Fink, I'm a keelboat poler
> I'm a Salt River roarer and I eat live coals
> I'm a half-alligator and I ride tornaders
> And I can out-feather, out-jump, out-hop, out-skip
> Throw down and lick any man on the river.
> Well I poled the Ohio and I poled the Mississippi
> And I poled the Missouri when she's choked with snags
> I poled on the wilds and the salts of the Kentucky
> And I never met a man that I couldn't out-brag.[3]

More often, tall tales are about made-up characters. Some were told by cowboys around the campfire, and others were written for publication. One fictional hero was named Pecos Bill, created by Edward O'Reilly. It was said that, as a baby, he fell out of his parent's wagon and was raised by coyotes. When he grew up, Pecos Bill rode a mountain lion and used a live rattlesnake as a whip. No one else could ride his horse, named Widow-Maker. Bill's bride, Slue-Foot Sue, was also adventurous. They met when she came riding down the Rio Grande on a catfish said to be as big as a whale.

Tall tales about the mighty lumberman Paul Bunyan and his blue ox, Babe, were written to advertise the Red River Lumber Company. According to those stories, Bunyan's footprints

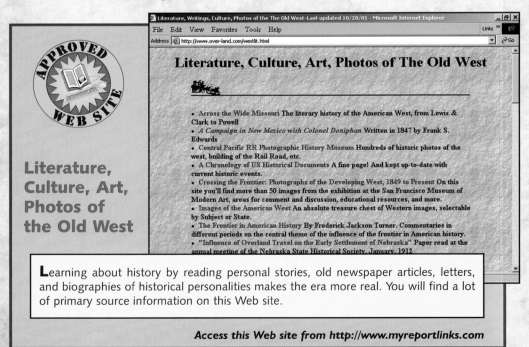

Literature, Culture, Art, Photos of the Old West

Literature, Writings, Culture, Photos of the The Old West-Last updated 10/28/01 - Microsoft Internet Explorer

File   Edit   View   Favorites   Tools   Help

Address http://www.over-land.com/westlit.html

Literature, Culture, Art, Photos of The Old West

• Across the Wide Missouri The literary history of the American West, from Lewis & Clark to Powell
• A Campaign in New Mexico with Colonel Doniphan Written in 1847 by Frank S. Edwards
• Central Pacific RR Photographic History Museum Hundreds of historic photos of the west, building of the Rail Road, etc.
• A Chronology of US Historical Documents A fine page! And kept up-to-date with current historic events.
• Crossing the Frontier: Photographs of the Developing West, 1849 to Present On this site you'll find more than 50 images from the exhibition at the San Francisco Museum of Modern Art, areas for comment and discussion, educational resources, and more.
• Images of the American West An absolute treasure chest of Western images, selectable by Subject or State.
• The Frontier in American History By Frederick Jackson Turner. Commentaries in different periods on the central theme of the influence of the frontier in American history.
• "Influence of Overland Travel on the Early Settlement of Nebraska" Paper read at the annual meeting of the Nebraska State Historical Society, January, 1912

Learning about history by reading personal stories, old newspaper articles, letters, and biographies of historical personalities makes the era more real. You will find a lot of primary source information on this Web site.

Access this Web site from http://www.myreportlinks.com

created Minnesota's ten thousand lakes. And when Bunyan dragged his axe along as he walked, the result was the Grand Canyon.

Story Newspapers and Dime Novels

Nineteenth-century illustrated newspapers and magazines ran pictures and descriptions of colorful western life. Their detailed images of cowboys and American Indians were printed from etched copper plates called engravings. Publications such as Frank Leslie's *Illustrated Newspaper,* *The New York Saturday Press,* and *Harper's Weekly* magazines brought the Wild West to eastern readers.

Weekly papers such as *The New York Ledger and Saturday Night* featured series of stories, poems, humor, fashion, and current events. Also called "six-cent weeklies," they were very popular as family entertainment. Some sold as many as four hundred thousand copies per issue.[4] The stories were about romances, outlaws, detectives, and adventures in the Wild West.

Dime novels carried similar tales. These very popular paperback books were sold at newsstands and in general stores. Like the illustrated papers, dime novels presented an exciting—but seldom absolutely true—picture of western life. They were popular from about 1860 to 1910. Most were about one hundred pages and had an illustration of some action scene on the cover.[5]

A New York writer who called himself Ned Buntline had a talent for making the unlikely and the impossible sound real. And Buntline was a fast writer. He could turn out two dime novels every week.[6] His real name was Edward Zane Carroll Judson, and he had been a sailor, con man, horse thief, soldier, writer, and editor.[7] He found fame and fortune as the author of popular dime novels, especially those about Buffalo Bill Cody.

Although Buntline wrote about the Wild West, he seldom actually went there. In 1869, on one of only two trips west, he met William F. Cody. They would make each other famous.

Wild West Stories

William F. Cody was a real westerner. Before he reached twenty-one, he earned the name Buffalo Bill for his work as a hunter supplying meat to the Kansas Pacific Railroad. By the late 1860s, Cody was on his way to becoming a showman.

At that time, celebrities and other wealthy easterners loved to go on buffalo hunts. Somebody had to organize those hunts to make sure the celebrity survived and actually killed a buffalo. Bill Cody had a charming personality and got along well with the would-be hunters. He was often called upon for the job.

THE FOOD OF OUR YOUTH.

Dime novels often told fantastic stories of the exploits of men and women in the Wild West. Oftentimes these stories were untrue, yet they made for exciting reading. This cartoon warns against the harmful affects that the illustrator feels dime novels had on young people of the time.

When Buntline went west in 1869, he was looking for a western hero to write about. He found William F. Cody, who was tall, good-looking, and charming. Buntline would have no problems making up suitable stories about him.

On December 23, 1869, *The New York Weekly* ran the first part of a new series "Buffalo Bill, the King of the Border Men."[8] In Buntline's story, Buffalo Bill charged out of nowhere, riding a great white stallion. He always rescued whoever needed rescuing. The first printing sold out in a week, and eager readers bought over a million copies. Lots of other authors began turning out dime-novel Westerns.

Buffalo Bill Cody made no money from Buntline's book, although the publicity did increase his guide business. In 1872, the Grand Duke Alexis of Russia hired Buffalo Bill Cody to take him on a three-day hunting trip. What followed was more like a performance than an actual hunt.

▶ The Grand Duke's Buffalo Hunt

By the time the Grand Duke Alexis arrived on his special train, Cody had arranged for some of his American Indian friends to put on a special show. Spotted Tail, the leader of a Sioux tribe, and his braves wore their war paint and performed a war dance. Then Buffalo Bill took the duke hunting.

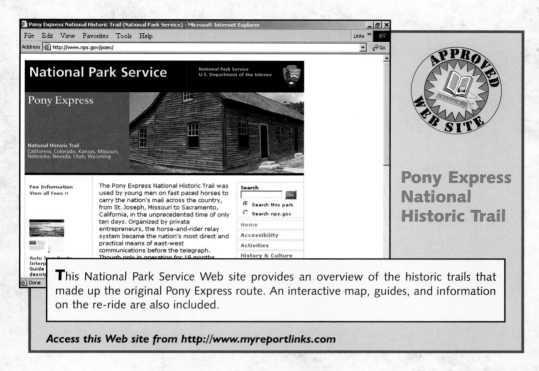

Pony Express National Historic Trail (National Park Service) - Microsoft Internet Explorer

File   Edit   View   Favorites   Tools   Help   Links »

Address http://www.nps.gov/poex/   Go

National Park Service   National Park Service
                                   U.S. Department of the Interior

Pony Express

National Historic Trail
California, Colorado, Kansas, Missouri,
Nebraska, Nevada, Utah, Wyoming

Fee Information   The Pony Express National Historic Trail was   Search
View all Fees »   used by young men on fast paced horses to   Go
                        carry the nation's mail across the country,   ⦿ Search this park
                        from St. Joseph, Missouri to Sacramento,   ○ Search nps.gov
                        California, in the unprecedented time of only
                        ten days. Organized by private   Home
                        entrepreneurs, the horse-and-rider relay   Accessibility
                        system became the nation's most direct and
                        practical means of east-west   Activities
                        communications before the telegraph.   History & Culture
                        Though only in operation for 18 months

Auto Town Route
Interp
Guide
descrip

**Pony Express
National
Historic Trail**

This National Park Service Web site provides an overview of the historic trails that made up the original Pony Express route. An interactive map, guides, and information on the re-ride are also included.

Access this Web site from http://www.myreportlinks.com

According to Pulitzer prize-winning author and American West expert Larry McMurtry, the duke was no marksman:

> By some accounts the Grand Duke was so myopic [near-sighted] that he shot two or three horses before they could get him pointed toward the buffalo. Cody's own account of this awkward hunt was of course more discreet, but he does admit that he had to lend the Grand Duke his best horse and his favorite rifle . . . and do everything but pull the trigger for him before a buffalo could be induced to fall—and he may even have pulled the trigger.[9]

The whole thing became a media event—just like celebrity activities are today. Newspapers back east eagerly wrote up the story. Newspaper readers were delighted to discover that their favorite dime-novel hero really existed. Then, Buffalo Bill's popularity gave one playwright a new idea—and led Cody into a new career.

▶ On Stage

In February 1872, a new play titled *Buffalo Bill, the King of the Border Men* opened in New York City. It was written by Fred G. Maeder and based on Ned Buntline's book. Actor J. B. Studley played the role of Buffalo Bill.

While the play was running, Bill Cody visited New York for the first time. Dressed up in his fringed buckskin suit, Cody went with Buntline to see the play. Before long, the audience realized that the real Buffalo Bill was in the audience. He was persuaded to go up on stage and take a bow. Buffalo Bill Cody was a hit. The theater manager offered him five hundred dollars a week to play himself on stage. But Cody was eager to get back to the West and his own real life, so he turned the part down.

A few months later, Cody needed money. The winter had been hard on his hunting expeditions, and his wife had given birth to their third child.[10] That December, William Cody and another western scout, John Burwell Omohundro, went to Chicago to meet with Ned Buntline. Buntline had written about Omohundro as "Texas Jack." With the arrival of the two heroes, the Chicago theater manager was ready to go ahead with a play. He wanted to open it in just a few days.

Buntline had not yet written the play, but he turned it out in four hours. He rehearsed Buffalo Bill and Texas Jack in their roles for three days. They opened *The Scouts of the Prairie* to an audience of twenty-five hundred. Hundreds more had been turned away for lack of space. The play got terrible reviews, but still attracted huge audiences. To the playgoers, it was their chance to see the "real" Wild West.

Reality Show and Improv

Cody was twenty-six years old and still shy in front of a crowd. He was awkward on stage. He could not remember his lines. He admitted that they never actually performed the script that Buntline had written in such a hurry. But audiences seemed happy with whatever their heroes had to say. Their favorite dime novel had been brought to life on the stage.

The play was an odd combination of things. One actress playing an American Indian princess sang a number from a popular European opera. Another actress, also playing an American Indian princess, spoke with a heavy Italian accent. Ned Buntline was in the cast, and he would occasionally

Buffalo Bill toured around the country with his Wild West Show. The show featured legendary cowboys, women, and American Indians of the Old West performing skits and showing off their skills.

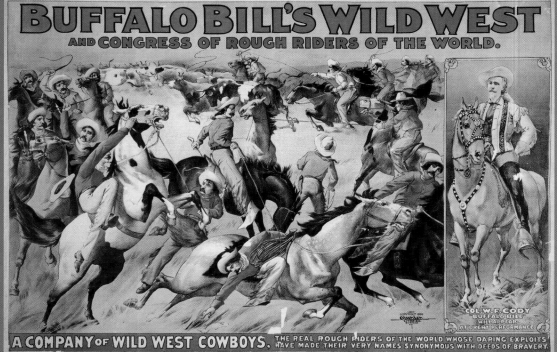

stop the action with one of his lectures against drinking alcohol. Much was improvised, and some was what today might be called a reality show.

After Chicago, *The Scouts of the Prairie* toured other cities. In St. Louis, Missouri, Cody's mother came to see the show. She reported that her son spotted her in the audience:

> He came forward, leaned over the gas footlights, and waved his arms.
>
> "Oh, Mamma!" he shouted, "I'm a bad actor." The house roared. Will threw me a kiss and then leaned forward again, while the house stilled.
>
> "Honest, Mamma," he shouted, "does this look as awful out there as it feels up here?"[11]

Buffalo Bill insisted that his mother come on stage, saying, "You can't be any worse scared than I am."[12]

In 1873, Fred G. Maeder wrote a new play, *The Scouts of the Plains*. In addition to Buffalo Bill and Texas Jack, the characters included Wild Bill Hickok. James Butler Hickok was also a real western scout who became famous in dime novels. But Hickok never took to acting very well. Shooting out the spotlight was just one of the times that he fired his guns on stage in front of a live audience.

Wild Bill did not stay with the stage troupe for very long, but Buffalo Bill and Texas Jack went on to do other shows. In the summer, they usually went back to their scouting jobs for the army. In

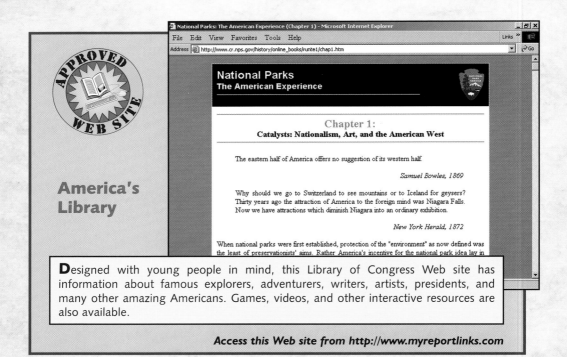

National Parks: The American Experience (Chapter 1) - Microsoft Internet Explorer

File　Edit　View　Favorites　Tools　Help

Address http://www.cr.nps.gov/history/online_books/runte1/chap1.htm

National Parks
The American Experience

Chapter 1:
Catalysts: Nationalism, Art, and the American West

The eastern half of America offers no suggestion of its western half.

Samuel Bowles, 1869

Why should we go to Switzerland to see mountains or to Iceland for geysers?
Thirty years ago the attraction of America to the foreign mind was Niagara Falls.
Now we have attractions which diminish Niagara into an ordinary exhibition.

New York Herald, 1872

When national parks were first established, protection of the "environment" as now defined was
the least of preservationists' aims. Rather America's incentive for the national park idea lay in

America's Library

Designed with young people in mind, this Library of Congress Web site has information about famous explorers, adventurers, writers, artists, presidents, and many other amazing Americans. Games, videos, and other interactive resources are also available.

Access this Web site from http://www.myreportlinks.com

the winter, they returned to the stage. Buffalo Bill Cody would later put on his own Wild West shows.

People came to believe that the West was like the stories told in print and on stage. Those stories defined American heroes. They described how honorable men should behave. And in the shows, women had roles as strong and independent characters who made their own decisions. The players were real people, and most of them were real Westerners.

Chapter 2

FROM WILDERNESS TO WILD WEST

Before there was a Wild West, there was just a western wilderness. At least, that is how most Americans thought about the whole area between the Mississippi River and the Pacific Ocean. Toward the end of the 1700s, many Americans believed that the Mississippi was the natural western boundary of the United States. Everything beyond the Mississippi seemed useless and dangerous.

In 1820, the Army Corps of Engineers sent an expedition along the Platte River. Major Stephen Long reported back that the Great Plains were "unfit for cultivation and of course uninhabitable by a people depending upon agriculture." On his map of the area, he labeled it a "Great Desert."[1] Frontiersman Zebulon Pike referred to this area as "The Great American Desert" in 1806–07.

Of course, people already lived in that part of the continent. They had been there for twenty thousand years or more.

▶ American Indians

Long ago, groups of people traveled to the Americas by way of a land bridge from Asia. They

▲ At first, the Great Plains was known as the Great Desert because Easterners thought it would be uninhabitable. American Indian tribes had been living on the Plains for thousands of years. This image is of a prairie in Wyoming.

settled in all parts of the North and South American continents. They came to call themselves by a variety of names—Algonquin, Cherokee, Iroquois, Sioux, Shoshone, Navajo, Hopi, and many others. Today, a lot of places are still named after those original residents—Dakota, Iowa, Kansas, Pima, Cheyenne, Omaha, Missouri, and Illinois, to mention just a few.

Some of these tribes, or nations, were friends, some were trading partners, some fought each other, and some had little or no contact with any others. They spoke different languages and told different stories about how the world came to be and why their people lived where they did. They developed their own ceremonies and traditions.

When explorers from Europe reached their lands, things began to change for American Indians. One hundred years after Spanish explorers brought horses into the West, American Indians owned thousands of horses and were among the most skilled riders of all time. Eventually, they would find themselves living in America's Wild West.

Early Spanish Influence

In the mid-1500s, Spanish explorers searched the American West for seven legendary cities of gold. Spaniards started building missions, towns, and forts in Florida in the mid-1500s, in Texas and New Mexico in the mid-1600s, and along the California coast in the mid-1700s. They wanted to convert natives to Christianity and to gain land for Spain.

These early explorers, priests, settlers, and soldiers brought Spanish horses and longhorn cattle with them. The descendents of those Spanish horses and longhorn cattle would help shape the Wild West.

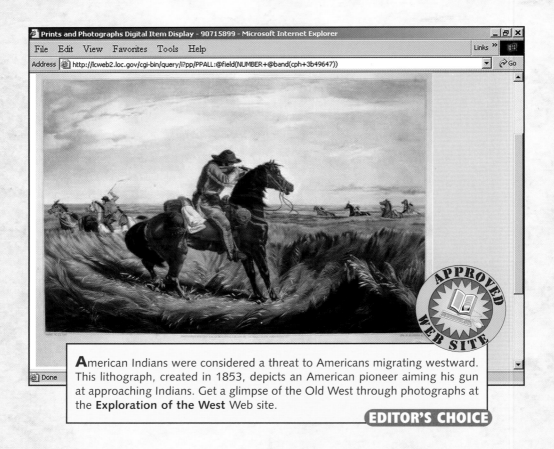

Prints and Photographs Digital Item Display - 90715899 - Microsoft Internet Explorer

File   Edit   View   Favorites   Tools   Help   Links »

Address   http://lcweb2.loc.gov/cgi-bin/query/i?pp/PPALL:@field(NUMBER+@band(cph+3b49647))   Go

Done

American Indians were considered a threat to Americans migrating westward. This lithograph, created in 1853, depicts an American pioneer aiming his gun at approaching Indians. Get a glimpse of the Old West through photographs at the **Exploration of the West** Web site.

APPROVED WEB SITE

EDITOR'S CHOICE

The Fur Trade

Even when the West was still considered a wilderness, some Americans made money working there. Furs were among the first things that Americans could sell to Europeans for cash.

"Long hunters" shot deer for their hides. In the 1760s, Daniel Boone was a long hunter on the frontier of his time—the Kentucky wilderness. A tanned deerskin was soft enough to use for making clothing called buckskins. The skin of a doe (female deer) was worth about fifty cents. The hide of a buck (male deer) brought a dollar or more. That is how the word "buck" became slang for a dollar.[2] Small bands of hunters could get hundreds of deerskins in a hunting season.

When steamboats came into use on the Missouri River in the 1830s, buffalo robes became popular dress among Americans and Europeans. American Indians brought their buffalo hides and robes to trading posts on the upper Missouri. Traders exchanged woven fabrics, blankets, knives, guns, powder, lead, and tobacco for the hides. Then the traders shipped the furs down the river to markets in St. Louis.

About the same time, men's tall beaver hats were in great demand in eastern cities, in England and other parts of Europe. Beaver hats were naturally waterproof, and they held their shape. Beaver pelts brought a good price, and they became favorites with trappers. In the 1700s, fur trappers found beaver near the Great Lakes. But soon, trappers would head even farther west.

▶ Into the West

In 1803, President Thomas Jefferson bought a huge part of the wilderness for the United States. It was called the Louisiana Territory. In 1804, the president sent Meriwether Lewis and William Clark with a team to explore the new purchase. When Lewis and Clark got back to the East in

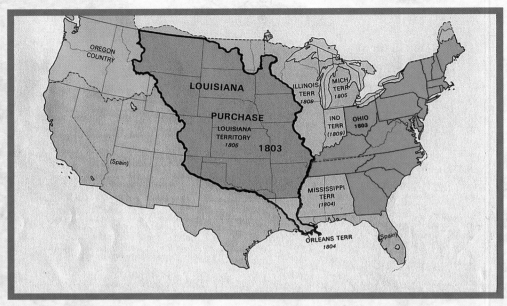

This map shows the borders of the United States in 1810 after the Louisiana Purchase. The land obtained in that deal is shown in the center.

1806, they reported on the geography and American Indian inhabitants of the territory.

Lewis and Clark also reported that there was a rich supply of beavers in western rivers. A few trappers had been roaming the western mountains even before that news. Now more headed for that area.

These trappers became known as "mountain men." Many lived alone, far from any town, and owned nothing that they could not carry with them. They lived off the land as they roamed hundreds of miles in search of beaver pelts. The mountain men were explorers as well as trappers. As they hunted for skins, they broke new trails.

And they also saw some remarkable sights. Here are a few of their names and stories.

The Adventures of Mountain Men

African-American scout and fur trapper Jim Beckwourth discovered a pass suitable for wagons in the Sierra Nevada Mountains of California. He reported that "Swarms of wild geese and ducks were swimming on the surface of the cool crystal stream. . . . Deer and antelope filled the plains . . . and it is probable that our steps were the first that ever marked this spot."[3] Beckwourth later became a chief of the Crow Nation.

John Colter was a member of Lewis and Clark's expedition team. On the trip home, Colter left the expedition to join a group of trappers. Later, wandering on his own, he found a place where hot water shot up out of the ground into the air. Even the earth bubbled like boiling water. When Colter reported what he had seen, everyone thought it was just another tall tale. Today, the place he found is known as Yellowstone National Park, and the geyser called Old Faithful is one of the park's most popular attractions.[4]

Jim Bridger started trapping in 1822, at the age of eighteen. Sometimes he worked with others, sometimes alone. In 1824, Bridger came across a huge body of saltwater. At first, he

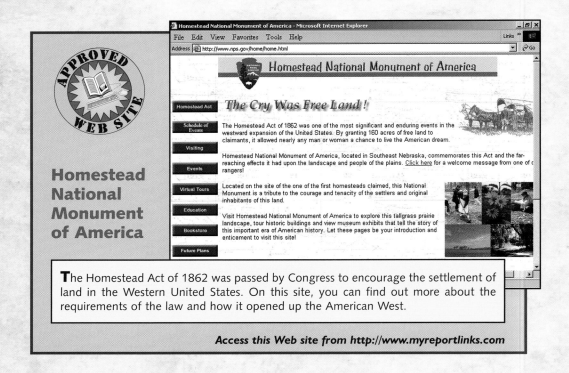

Homestead National Monument of America - Microsoft Internet Explorer

File   Edit   View   Favorites   Tools   Help   Links »

Address http://www.nps.gov/home/home.html   Go

Homestead National Monument of America

The Cry Was Free Land!

The Homestead Act of 1862 was one of the most significant and enduring events in the westward expansion of the United States. By granting 160 acres of free land to claimants, it allowed nearly any man or woman a chance to live the American dream.

Homestead National Monument of America, located in Southeast Nebraska, commemorates this Act and the far-reaching effects it had upon the landscape and people of the plains. Click here for a welcome message from one of our rangers!

Located on the site of the one of the first homesteads claimed, this National Monument is a tribute to the courage and tenacity of the settlers and original inhabitants of this land.

Visit Homestead National Monument of America to explore this tallgrass prairie landscape, tour historic buildings and view museum exhibits that tell the story of this important era of American history. Let these pages be your introduction and enticement to visit this site!

Homestead Act · Schedule of Events · Visiting · Events · Virtual Tours · Education · Bookstore · Future Plans

Homestead National Monument of America

The Homestead Act of 1862 was passed by Congress to encourage the settlement of land in the Western United States. On this site, you can find out more about the requirements of the law and how it opened up the American West.

Access this Web site from http://www.myreportlinks.com

thought he had reached the Pacific Ocean. But instead, Bridger had found the Great Salt Lake.

Jedediah Smith was also a fur trader and an explorer. Smith became one of the most famous of the mountain men. He wandered the West for forty years—from Canada to Mexico—and came to know the territory well. The maps he drew would be the best ones available to settlers of the West for over twenty years.[5]

These mountain men were very tough. Jim Bridger was hit in the back with an arrow, and the arrowhead stayed there for three years. Bridger finally had it cut out, but without anything to numb the pain.

Jedediah Smith ran across another constant danger to the mountain men—a grizzly bear. The bear broke Smith's ribs, tore off part of his scalp, and nearly tore off an ear during a struggle. Smith directed a companion, James Clyman, to sew him back together. Clyman said, "I put in my needle, stitching it through and through and over and over, laying the lacerated [cut] parts together as nice as I could."[6]

John Colter was once captured by American Indians in the area that is now Montana. The Blackfoot warriors stripped him and gave him a chance to run for his life. Colter ran. He raced to the Madison River, dove in, and hid under a

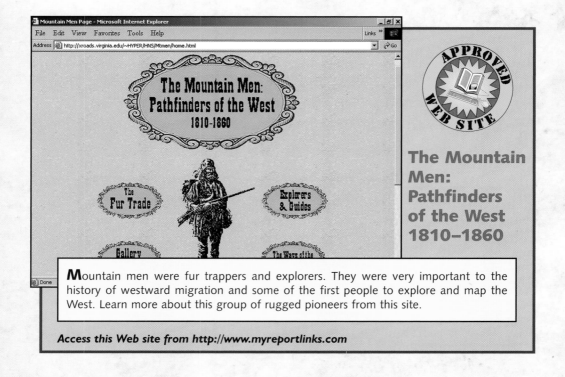

The Mountain Men: Pathfinders of the West 1810–1860

Mountain men were fur trappers and explorers. They were very important to the history of westward migration and some of the first people to explore and map the West. Learn more about this group of rugged pioneers from this site.

Access this Web site from http://www.myreportlinks.com

beaver dam. That night he came out of the water and ran for another eleven days—naked, barefoot, and bleeding. He lived off of roots, grubs, and tree bark. Colter finally reached safety at a fort on the Bighorn River, about two hundred miles from the Madison. Soon after that, he retired to a safer life in St. Louis.

Rendezvous

In 1822, William Ashley and Andrew Henry organized a new system for trappers. Ashley advertised in a St. Louis paper for a hundred "Enterprising Young Men" to work for the Rocky Mountain Fur Company. He had no problem signing up a hundred men. At various times, Smith, Bridger, and Mike Fink worked with the Rocky Mountain company.

These trappers went up into the mountains on horseback in groups. Once a year, the trappers would bring their pelts to a rendezvous. (Rendezvous is a French word for a meeting planned for a certain time and place.) From the rendezvous, the buyers hauled the furs to markets by mule train and wagon. The trappers stayed in the mountains.

The rendezvous quickly became more than just a place to sell furs. It developed into a month-long event with horse races, footraces, target shooting, and gambling.

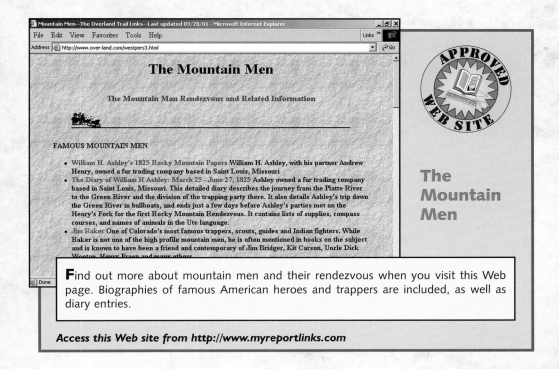

Mountain Men--The Overland Trail Links--Last updated 03/20/01 - Microsoft Internet Explorer

File   Edit   View   Favorites   Tools   Help   Links »

Address http://www.over-land.com/westpers3.html   Go

The Mountain Men

The Mountain Man Rendezvous and Related Information

FAMOUS MOUNTAIN MEN

- William H. Ashley's 1825 Rocky Mountain Papers William H. Ashley, with his partner Andrew Henry, owned a fur trading company based in Saint Louis, Missouri
- The Diary of William H Ashley: March 25 - June 27, 1825 Ashley owned a fur trading company based in Saint Louis, Missouri. This detailed diary describes the journey from the Platte River to the Green River and the division of the trapping party there. It also details Ashley's trip down the Green River in bullboats, and ends just a few days before Ashley's parties met on the Henry's Fork for the first Rocky Mountain Rendezvous. It contains lists of supplies, compass courses, and names of animals in the Ute language.
- Jim Baker One of Colorado's most famous trappers, scouts, guides and Indian fighters. While Baker is not one of the high profile mountain men, he is often mentioned in books on the subject and is known to have been a friend and contemporary of Jim Bridger, Kit Carson, Uncle Dick Wooton, Henry Fraen and many others.

The
Mountain
Men

Done

Find out more about mountain men and their rendezvous when you visit this Web page. Biographies of famous American heroes and trappers are included, as well as diary entries.

Access this Web site from http://www.myreportlinks.com

Other travelers came to join the party, including women and children, American Indians, and French Canadians.

Jim Beckwourth described the festivities at the rendezvous as a scene of "mirth, songs, dancing, shouting, trading, running, jumping, singing, racing, target-shooting, yarns, frolic, with all sorts of extravagances that white men or Indians could invent."[7] In other words, a rendezvous was very much like what we think of as the Wild West.

The Rocky Mountain men met for their last rendezvous in 1840. By then, there were fewer beavers left to trap, and styles were changing. Europeans had lost interest in beaver hats.

▲ Jim Bridger built Fort Bridger (shown here) on the banks of the Green River in what was then known as the Utah Territory.

▶ Legendary Trail Guides Lead the Way

Mountain men helped others reach the Far West. For example, Jedediah Smith led the first group of Americans overland to California in 1826. In 1843, Jim Bridger built a fort on the Green River in Wyoming Territory that was named Fort Bridger. It became a popular stopping place for settlers migrating west. Bridger also guided prospectors to mines and laid out roads for stage-coach routes. In 1865, he helped surveyors work out a route for the Union Pacific Railroad.

Trail guide Kit Carson was also a legendary trailblazer. In 1826, at age fifteen, Carson ran away from Missouri and got a job with a hunting party. That was the beginning of his long career as a scout and guide.

Like Buffalo Bill Cody and Wild Bill Hickok, Kit Carson became a dime-novel hero. In 1849, one of those novels turned up at the scene of a tragedy. An American Indian Apache raiding party attacked a family on the Santa Fe Trail. They killed the husband and carried off his wife.

Kit Carson led a military party to the raiders, but the kidnappers killed Mrs. White and fled. Carson was sad that he had come to her rescue too late. He was even more upset about the dime novel he found at the scene. Kit Carson could not read or write. Someone had to tell him what the novel was about. He reported it later:

> In the camp was found a book, the first of the kind that I had ever seen, in which I was made a great hero, slaying Indians by the hundreds and I have often thought that Mrs. White would read the same and knowing that I lived near, she would pray for my appearance and that she might be saved.[8]

Like the other heroes of the Wild West, Kit Carson was not a superman. He did his best, and sometimes it was not enough.

Learning to Love the Wilderness

By treaty and by war, America came to own the western wilderness. In 1846, a treaty with Great

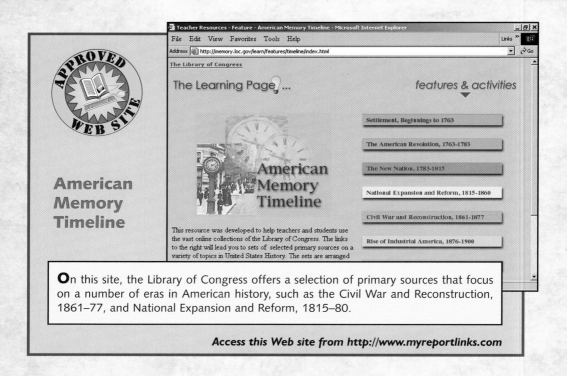

The Library of Congress

The Learning Page ...

features & activities

American
Memory
Timeline

Settlement, Beginnings to 1763

The American Revolution, 1763-1783

The New Nation, 1783-1815

National Expansion and Reform, 1815-1860

Civil War and Reconstruction, 1861-1877

Rise of Industrial America, 1876-1900

This resource was developed to help teachers and students use the vast online collections of the Library of Congress. The links to the right will lead you to sets of selected primary sources on a variety of topics in United States History. The sets are arranged

On this site, the Library of Congress offers a selection of primary sources that focus on a number of eras in American history, such as the Civil War and Reconstruction, 1861–77, and National Expansion and Reform, 1815–80.

Access this Web site from http://www.myreportlinks.com

Britain set the northwest boundary with Canada where it is in 2006. In 1836, Texas declared its independence from Mexico, and in 1845 Texas became part of the United States. The outcome of the 1846–48 Mexican-American War gained California and the Southwest for the United States.

By 1850, a map of the United States looked very much as it does today. In 1851, *New York Tribune* editor Horace Greeley made "Go west young man!" a favorite American saying. Greeley had picked up the line from an editorial in the *Terre Haute Express,* in which John L. Soule wrote, "Go West, young man, and grow up with the country."

Horace Greeley was a famous editor of the New York Tribune *newspaper. The paper's articles helped inspire young men and families to seek their fortune in the West.*

American author Henry David Thoreau spent two years living in a small cabin in the Massachusetts woods. Although Thoreau never traveled to the West, he thought of that as the direction of the future. Thoreau took daily walks in Massachusetts, but he was thinking about the American West. He wrote:

> Eastward I go only by force; but westward I go free. . . . I must walk toward Oregon, and not toward Europe. And that way the nation is moving. . . . The West of which I speak is but another name for the Wild; and what I have been preparing to say is, that in Wildness is the preservation of the World.[9]

American attitudes about the wilderness—that Great Desert—were changing.

LEGENDS, LAND, AND GOLD

During the 1800s, the American wilderness became the Wild West. Exciting stories, new land, and the possibility of wealth all drew more Americans westward.

The hit novel of the 1820s was James Fenimore Cooper's *The Last of the Mohicans,* the story of a fictional frontiersmen called Natty Bumppo. Cooper's work was based on childhood experiences in New York State's western frontier—and on his own active imagination.

Author Samuel Clemens also made the West seem irresistible with tales he wrote under the name Mark Twain. "The Celebrated Jumping Frog of Calaveras County" is Twain's original tall tale about life in a California mining camp. Bret Harte did the same, writing about humorous western characters in "The Luck of Roaring Camp."

▶ The Power of Pictures

Artists also helped to pull people westward. In the early 1820s, John J. Audubon went on a quest to discover America's birds. With his art materials, a gun, and one assistant, Audubon floated down the Mississippi, drawing and painting. His book, *The Birds of America,* aroused interest in America's wildlife.

Beginning in 1832, artist George Catlin traveled 2,000 miles with trappers from the American Fur Company. He painted hundreds of portraits of American Indians, which he exhibited in Europe as well as in America. The following year, painter Karl Bodmer also went west and recorded scenes of American Indian life firsthand.

John James Audubon

John James Audubon is a famous bird enthusiast and naturalist whose legacy lives on in the National Audubon Society, which works to conserve the ecosystems of birds. Read a biography of John James Audubon on the **John James Audubon** Web site.

In 1859, Albert Bierstadt's large canvases of the Rocky Mountains and the Yosemite area impressed easterners and Europeans with the beauties of the West. Later in the century, artist Frederic Remington spent time in the Arizona Territory, recording the United States cavalry and American Indian Apaches led by the warrior Geronimo.

The wilderness came to be seen as a place of beauty, adventure, and opportunity for those who were up to the challenges it presented.

▶ Settling the West

Many people in the eastern part of the country were eager to own land. They wanted to make a new start in a place where they could support themselves. When they learned that there was good grazing and farming land in the West, families loaded up their belongings and set out on a dangerous journey.

In 1841, the first wagon train of pioneers crossed the Rocky Mountains. Nearly one thousand settlers made that first trip to Oregon and northern California, driving a herd of five thousand cattle.[1] Thousands more people would travel the Oregon Trail during the following years. It was known as the "Great Migration."

The journey from Independence, Missouri, to the green pastures of California and Oregon was

California History Collection - Microsoft Internet Explorer

File   Edit   View   Favorites   Tools   Help   Links »

Address | http://memory.loc.gov/ammem/cbhtml/cbintro.html   ▼ ℰGo

Introduction

Early California History: An Overview

Table of Contents

Early California History: An Overview

Read an essay containing an abundance of information about early California history at this Library of Congress Web site. Find out how California became the Golden State.

Access this Web site from http://www.myreportlinks.com

about two thousand miles. Some historians believe that one person in ten died on the way; others place that number higher.[2] According to the Oregon-California Trails Association, a "conservative figure is 20,000 for the entire two thousand miles of California Trail, or an average of ten graves to each mile."[3]

Most deaths along the trail were from cholera and other diseases caused by poor sanitation. But many travelers (especially children) died from accidents such as being run over by wagon wheels. Others died in firearm accidents, animal stampedes, violence between travelers, gunpowder explosions, lightning strikes, and by suicide. In some areas, American Indians were dangerous to the settlers; in other areas the natives were quite helpful.

▶ Gold!

In 1848, the California territory became part of the United States. That same year, a remarkable discovery made northern California a very important place.

▲ The discovery of gold at Sutter's Mill in California in 1848 led to a horde of Americans heading west to seek their fortunes. This painting by William Henry Jackson is the artist's rendition of James Marshall's discovery.

In January, James Marshall was building a sawmill for John Sutter, who owned a nearby fort and settlement. Marshall found something shiny in the water that flowed past the mill. It was gold. Although Sutter tried to keep the find secret, word soon got out.

When the news reached California towns, those towns emptied. According to Michael Johnson's *The Real West,* in Monterrey, "Workmen dropped their tools, soldiers threw down their rifles and deserted. A boarding-house keeper abandoned her guests and dashed off without collecting the money due to her."[4]

▶ Heading for the Hills

In San Francisco, two thirds of the population suddenly disappeared. One newspaper published its last story—about the discovery of gold—and closed down because the entire staff had left. Everyone had headed for the hills.

By the end of 1848, news of gold had made its way east. President Polk, eager to encourage settlement in the West, announced the discovery to the nation. In 1849, fortune hunters known as the "forty-niners" rushed to the goldfields by the thousands. According to Michael Johnson, "Americans, Mexicans, Indians, emigrants from all over Europe . . . brought to the goldfields a dozen languages and a thousand strange habits. . . ."

Old West Saloons Vintage Photographs - Microsoft Internet Explorer

File   Edit   View   Favorites   Tools   Help   Links »

Address http://www.legendsofamerica.com/PicturePages/PP-Saloon7-StockmanSaloonCo.html   Go

Old West Legends
Outlaw Legends
Photo Galleries
Roadside Attractions
Rocky Mtn Store
Route 66
Travel Destinations
Treasure Tales

ROCKY MOUNTAIN
GENERAL STORE

E-mail Us
Forums
Free Newsletter
Guestbook
Legends Blog
Links
Site
Su
Su

<< Previous 1 2 3 4 5 6 7 8 9 10 11 12 13 14 15 16 17 18 Next >>

Stockman's Saloon in Saguache, Colorado, 1920.

Courtesy Denver Public Library

Return to Old West Saloons

Saloons in the early days of the American West were a place where the mostly male clientele could drink and socialize. Sometimes it was also the only place where a man could get a shave and a haircut. **The Old West Legends: Adventures in the American West** Web site displays a large number of images and lots of information on the history of the Wild West.

EDITOR'S CHOICE

APPROVED WEB SITE

Forty-niners led a rough life. They might find a fortune under any clod of dirt, or they might dig for a year and find nothing. They entertained themselves by gambling and drinking. Justice was often quick, brutal, and unofficial. Punishment for stealing gold might include one hundred lashes with a whip, a shaved head, and cropped ears.[5] There was not much stealing of gold in the camps, but there was plenty of fighting and other acts of violence.

The gold near Sutter's Mill was found in dirt and in streams. It could be washed out of sand,

and sometimes it could simply be picked up out of the water. Prospectors on those goldfields usually worked over a small area and moved on to another. In other parts of the West, gold, silver, and other minerals had to be mined from deeper in the earth.

Blue Gold

During the Gold Rush, those who sold things miners needed often did very well. Some grocery store and hardware store owners became richer than gold diggers. One man made his Gold Rush fortune by stitching up a new kind of pants.

In 1853, Levi Strauss moved from New York to San Francisco. With him, he brought canvas for use as tents and wagon covers. But he found a much better market for his sewing skills.

Miners needed trousers that would not wear out quickly, so Strauss began making and selling "Levi's" pants. He soon changed to a more comfortable fabric, a heavy blue denim that the French called "genes." Soon Levi's jeans were considered basic equipment for miners, and later for cowboys, too.

By Land and by Sea

Fortune seekers and settlers went west by any means they could. Some went by ship to Panama, crossed over the Isthmus of Panama by pack mule,

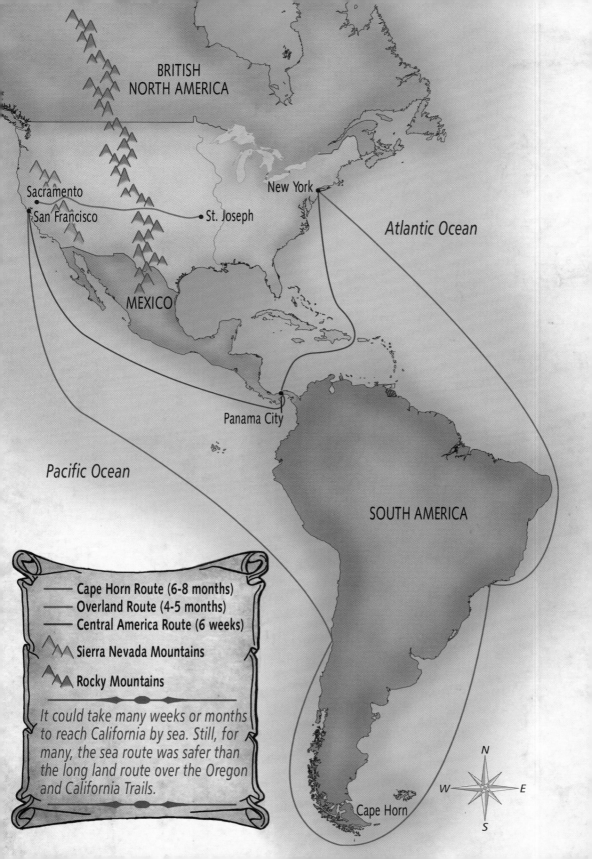

BRITISH
NORTH AMERICA

Sacramento

San Francisco

St. Joseph

New York

Atlantic Ocean

MEXICO

Panama City

Pacific Ocean

SOUTH AMERICA

Cape Horn

—— Cape Horn Route (6-8 months)
—— Overland Route (4-5 months)
—— Central America Route (6 weeks)

▲▲▲ Sierra Nevada Mountains

▲▲ Rocky Mountains

It could take many weeks or months to reach California by sea. Still, for many, the sea route was safer than the long land route over the Oregon and California Trails.

N
W   E
S

and took another ship north to San Francisco. Others took the longer sea route around Cape Horn at the tip of South America.

The sea routes were easier on the traveler than going by land, but they presented certain dangers. Travelers crossing Panama were exposed to diseases such as cholera and typhoid. Those sailing around the horn were often hit with storms. The sea routes were also more expensive.

Most people went to the West by land. Before trails were wide enough for wagons, they used trains of pack mules. Then they built all kinds of wheeled vehicles— two-wheeled carts drawn by oxen, wagons pulled by oxen or mules, and even two-wheeled handcarts pulled and pushed by human beings. The mules or wagons usually carried belongings and supplies. Most of the people walked all the way.

Between 1853 and 1860, a few people built wagons with huge sails. They hoped to cross the Great Plains using wind power. Some of these wind wagons actually worked. One in the Kansas Territory made it for 50 miles, passing hundreds of other travelers, before it overturned.

▶ Camel Power

In 1856, seventy-five seasick camels arrived in Indianola, Texas. The camels had been bought in the Middle East and shipped to Texas. Teams of

▲ Freight companies even tried using camels, like those pictured here, to carry goods in the 1800s. These particular animals are in their native Africa.

experienced camel drivers had been hired and brought along to manage them. But the camels did not get off to a good start in America. The sick animals caused such a stink that no one wanted to go near them.

When the camels recovered, a group of them were driven from Texas to Los Angeles, California. Some were used for work at an army post, some hauled freight, and a few were used by explorers.

However, mules and horses were frightened by the camels and human beings were not very keen on using them.

Most of the camels were sold to the highest bidder. Some wound up in a circus or lived out their lives on a ranch. Others were seen running wild in Idaho and western Montana, and rumors of camel sightings continued for another fifty or so years.

Neither sails nor camels moved many people or much freight. The public preferred to travel by ordinary stagecoaches, and later by extraordinary railroads.

Stagecoach Travel

In September 1858, John Butterfield's Overland Mail Company started mail and passenger service between St. Louis, Missouri, and San Francisco, California. By 1862, Butterfield's company became part of Wells, Fargo & Company. These companies ran large stagecoaches pulled by teams of four horses. They quickly became the most popular way to cross the country.

The coaches were often crowded, with people packed both inside and outside. Stagecoach travelers put up with dust, breakdowns, and runaway teams. If the stage got stuck in the mud, passengers had no choice but to get out and help push it.

Stagecoaches on long journeys traveled day and night, and the passengers slept sitting up. Every 10 or 15 miles, the coaches stopped to change horses and passengers could get out for a brief rest. Some of the stations were just shacks or

The stagecoach was a popular method of westward travel because it was inexpensive compared to the journey by sea. This is a painting called "The Old Stage Coach of the Plains," by Frederic Remington.

dugouts in the sides of hills. Other stations had kitchens and provided meals.

Stagecoach drivers had to hold three pairs of reins, usually in one hand while using the other for the whip or brake. Well-known drivers included Wyatt Earp, William Cody, and James Butler Hickok. Another was Charley Parkhurst, who was discovered—after death—to actually be Charlotte Parkhurst.[6] It is believed that she pretended to be a man because back then it was much easier for a man to get a decent job. Parkhurst voted in an election long before women in the United States were allowed to.

Passengers sometimes carried money or other valuables, and the coaches also hauled freight. Since Wells Fargo was also in the banking business, they transported money or gold bullion. Then, guards armed with double-barrel shotguns rode alongside the stage driver.

In spite of the guards, bandits held up stagecoaches. During the 1860s, "The familiar 'Throw out that Express box' could be heard on some 313 stagecoach holdups on an average year."[7] Private detectives were soon hired to track down the outlaws.

The Pony Express

In 1859, William H. Russell thought up a way to deliver the mail even faster than stagecoaches

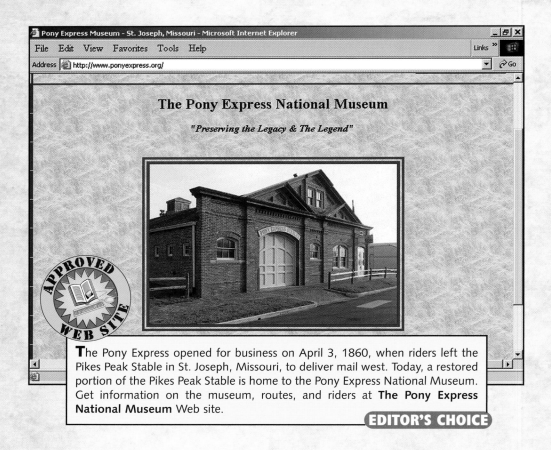

The Pony Express opened for business on April 3, 1860, when riders left the Pikes Peak Stable in St. Joseph, Missouri, to deliver mail west. Today, a restored portion of the Pikes Peak Stable is home to the Pony Express National Museum. Get information on the museum, routes, and riders at **The Pony Express National Museum** Web site.

could. Russell and his partner Alexander Majors bought about four hundred expensive, fast horses. Then they needed at least eighty excellent riders. They ran a newspaper ad that said exactly what they were looking for.

YOUNG, SKINNY, WIRY FELLOWS NOT OVER 18. MUST BE EXPERT RIDERS WILLING TO RISK DEATH DAILY. ORPHANS PREFERRED.[8]

Many young men answered the ad. When they were hired, riders had to take an oath not to use profane language, drink intoxicating liquors, or fight with any other employee. They promised to conduct themselves honestly and be faithful to their duties.

Most Pony Express riders were about twenty years old. Like today's racehorse jockeys, they had to be lightweight, but very strong and athletic. William F. Cody was a Pony Express rider. James Butler Hickok was hired to man one of the posts where the riders changed horses. They had yet to earn the nicknames Buffalo Bill or Wild Bill.

Cody, who was only fifteen, made one of the longest rides on record. When he discovered that his relief rider had been killed, Cody completed about three hundred miles in twenty-one hours and forty minutes, using twenty-one horses.[9]

A Brief History

In April 1860, the Pony Express started service over the 1,966 miles from St. Louis to Sacramento. At more than 150 stations, riders could change horses or fresh riders could take over. Riders covered about seventy-five miles. They got a fresh horse every 10 to 15 miles.

The Pony Express only operated until November 1861. By then transcontinental telegraph wires were sending messages from coast to coast. The Pony Express company never made any

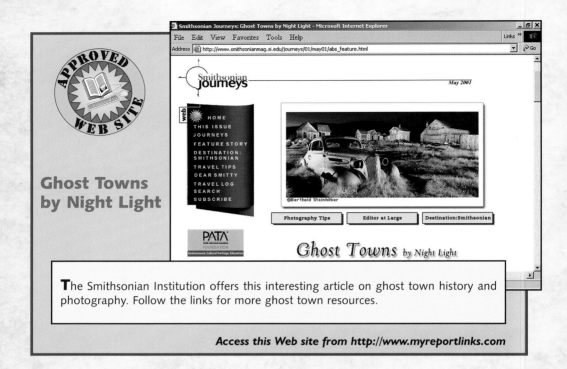

Ghost Towns by Night Light

The Smithsonian Institution offers this interesting article on ghost town history and photography. Follow the links for more ghost town resources.

Access this Web site from http://www.myreportlinks.com

money, but it became part of the great legends of the Wild West.

▶ Early Boomtowns

Towns naturally rose up along the wagon trails and stagecoach routes. Other settlements sprang up near gold, silver, and copper mines. If the minerals ran out, workers left and the settlements became ghost towns. If the mines were rich, people stayed and built better towns.

Gold and silver finds sent prospectors rushing to Nevada's Virginia City between 1859 and 1860 and to Montana's Last Chance Gulch in 1864. Other discoveries created other Wild West towns:

Deadwood, South Dakota; Tombstone, Arizona; and Cripple Creek, Colorado.

People living in some of those towns grew tired of the lawlessness and disorder often associated with mining towns. They began to organize to protect themselves and to improve their lifestyles. Vigilante groups (citizens acting as unofficial lawmen) ran troublemakers out of town. The townspeople also found and hired legal sheriffs.

▲ This painting shows cattle rustlers on the range catching a bear that had been terrorizing the livestock. This painting by C. M. Russell is called "Loops and Swift Horses are Surer Than Lead."

In those towns, people opened businesses and stayed even after the dream of sudden wealth had faded away. They built schools, churches, theaters, and libraries. They founded newspapers and organized entertainment ranging from prizefights to poetry readings.

The Beginning of the Cattle Business

The first cowboys spoke Spanish and called themselves *vaqueros* (vaca is Spanish for cow). They were Mexicans raising cattle in the northern Mexican provinces of Alta California and Tejas. When those lands became part of the United States, the cowboy tradition did, too. The Spanish letters "v" and "b" sound very much alike. American cowboys changed the word vaqueros— which sounded to them like ba-cah-rohs—to "buckaroos."

Western horses and cattle were descended from animals that had been brought to the New World by Spanish conquistadors in the 1500s. The horses, called mustangs, were not very large, but they were strong and tough. In the 1800s, wild herds of mustangs ran free in the West.

The cattle, a tough breed called longhorns, could also live in the wild. American settlers found more longhorn cattle in the West than anybody wanted to eat. At first they were rounded up for their hides and tallow (fat that could be used to

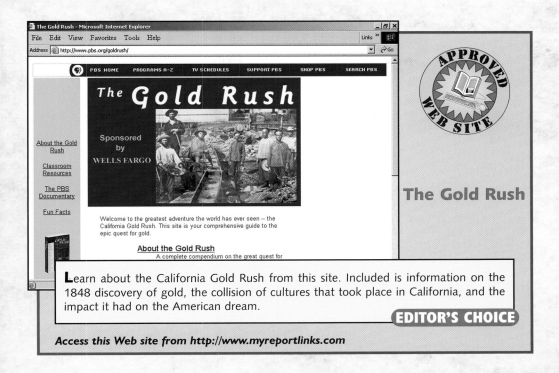

The Gold Rush

Learn about the California Gold Rush from this site. Included is information on the 1848 discovery of gold, the collision of cultures that took place in California, and the impact it had on the American dream.

EDITOR'S CHOICE

Access this Web site from http://www.myreportlinks.com

make candles and soap). During the Gold Rush, hungry forty-niners bought those that could be driven to California for meat.

In 1852, several cowboys drove about seven hundred steers from Texas to New York. The animals brought a good price, but that cattle drive took two years. By 1860, Texas cowboys had started driving herds of cattle to markets in St. Louis, Chicago, and other cities. Like most things in America, the cattle business was interrupted by the Civil War.

Chapter 4 ▶

COWBOYS, COWGIRLS, OUTLAWS, AND LAWMEN

From 1861 to 1865, the Union and the Confederacy fought the American Civil War. Even during that terrible war, President Abraham Lincoln did not forget about the West. He signed two bills that helped move people westward.

The Homestead Act gave settlers 160 acres of public land free if they lived there for five years. The Pacific Railroad Act gave two companies contracts to build a railroad that would cross the country. One company started in the East, the other started in the West. The Pacific Railroad Act also called for a telegraph line to be built alongside the rail line.

When the Civil War ended, thousands of former soldiers went looking for work. Freed slaves and new immigrants from Europe were also job hunting. The Union Pacific Railroad— the company building the eastern half of the Transcontinental Railroad—hired many of these men. Others went back to farming and ranching, or set up businesses in towns. And still others became cowboys.

▶ Cow Towns and Cattle Drives

When Texas farmers and ranchers returned home from the war, they found many more cattle than ever on the range. The cattle had multiplied, but there was no nearby market for beef. The Southern economy had been ruined by the war. What were they to do with all those longhorns?

New railroads stretching across the country helped in two ways: Railroad builders bought meat for their hundreds of workers, and railroads made it much easier to get cattle to eastern

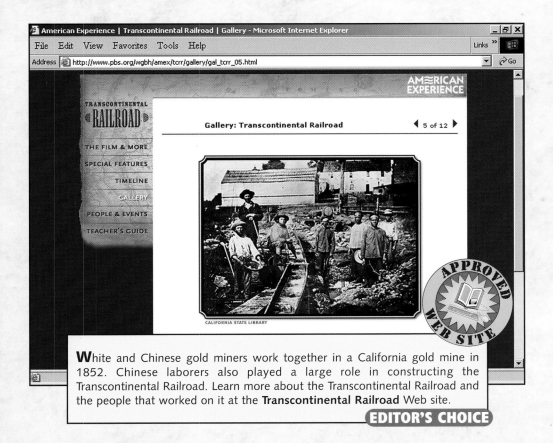

White and Chinese gold miners work together in a California gold mine in 1852. Chinese laborers also played a large role in constructing the Transcontinental Railroad. Learn more about the Transcontinental Railroad and the people that worked on it at the **Transcontinental Railroad** Web site.

EDITOR'S CHOICE

markets. Cowboys drove their herds of cattle along well-worn trails to railroad towns. The trails and the towns became famous. Perhaps the best example is the story of the Chisholm Trail.

Before the Civil War, part-Cherokee trader Jesse Chisholm had marked out a trail from Texas to Kansas. The wagon trail brought travelers to Chisholm's trading post near what is now Oklahoma City.

Joseph McCoy was a livestock trader in Chicago. In 1867, he persuaded Kansas Pacific Railroad officials to construct a train station at Abilene, Kansas. That year, about thirty-five thousand cattle were driven north from Texas along

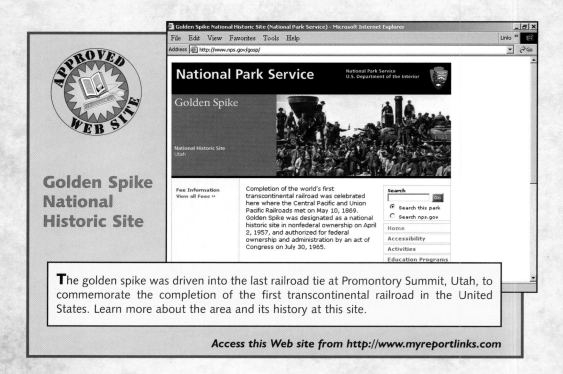

Golden Spike National Historic Site

The golden spike was driven into the last railroad tie at Promontory Summit, Utah, to commemorate the completion of the first transcontinental railroad in the United States. Learn more about the area and its history at this site.

Access this Web site from http://www.myreportlinks.com

the Chisholm Trail to Abilene. McCoy promised ranchers a good price for their cattle, and lived up to his word.

A trail boss was in charge of the cattle drive. He hired a dozen or more cowboys to drive the cattle and a wrangler to handle the 100 to 150 horses. The trail boss also hired a cook with a wagon, with provisions for meals along the way.

The herds were usually about twenty-five hundred to three thousand cattle, although some were as large as ten thousand animals. At the railroad town, the trail boss sold the cattle, paid the men, and took the profits back to Texas to the owner of the cattle.

Soon enough, Abilene became a prosperous cow town, a place where cowboys could relax after the long drive. Other cow towns also grew up around railroads and along well-worn trails.

Cowboys

American cowboys began to think of themselves as a special breed. They had real skills and they could handle the hardships of long drives over rough territory. They dressed in certain ways. They just did not look or behave like farmers or shopkeepers.

Most cowboys were young. Many had been Confederate soldiers from Texas. Others were veterans of the Union Army. About 15 percent of

10021563 - Microsoft Internet Explorer

File   Edit   View   Favorites   Tools   Help   Links »

Address http://photoswest.org/cgi-bin/imager?10021563+X-21563   Go

African-American cowboys played a large role in the cattle drives. Although they led a hard life, they often fared better than ex-slaves in other parts of the country. Black cowboys were often paid the same as white cowboys and in some cases, they were promoted to positions of power. Find out more at the **History of the American West, 1860–1920** Web site.

Done

cowboys were African American and some were Mexican American.[1] A few were women. For example, cowgirl Martha Jane Cannary became famous as Calamity Jane in dime novels and Wild West shows.

Many cowboys wore long blue or gray brass-buttoned army overcoats and still carried their military revolvers. At first, they wore ordinary work boots bought from general stores or from catalogs. But by the 1870s, most were using boots made especially for cowboys.

▶ Cowboy Gear

The narrow, pointy toes of cowboy boots could slide easily into stirrups. That meant the cowboy could get on or off a saddled horse quickly. High heels kept the boot from sliding all the way through the stirrup. That meant that if a cowboy fell off the horse, he would not get dragged around by one foot that had gotten stuck in a stirrup. The heels also helped the cowboy brace himself in the stirrups when he roped a horse or cow.

Cowboys wore Levi's jeans or other comfortable long pants. Over their pants went leather leg protectors called chaps. Their outfits were made for riding, not for foot travel. A cowboy seldom went far without his horse.

A cowboy's gear also included a good saddle, a lariat for roping, a neckerchief that could be pulled up when dust was blowing, and a hat. Wide-brimmed cowboy hats not only provided protection from the sun, they also might be used to fan a fire or scoop up water.

Most cowboys wore a revolver, usually the Colt Peacemaker. Many also carried a rifle in a leather scabbard (cover) on their saddle. The guns were useful for killing rattlesnakes, making enough noise to turn running cattle aside, or to signal if the cowboy needed help. Sometimes the six-shooter was left behind while a cowboy was working. But

▲ The life of the cowboy has been often imitated and glorified by American culture in the form of stories, movies, and country-and-western music.

when a cowboy went to town to celebrate the end of the drive, he usually wore his gun.[2]

American Indians

As Americans of European descent moved into the West, the United States government forced American Indians to move, again and again, usually to poorer territory. The government made treaties giving certain lands to tribes, but usually broke those treaties a decade or so later.

Some American Indian chiefs, such as the Lakota's Sitting Bull and Crazy Horse, refused to follow government orders to move to reservations. The battles that followed were brutal on both sides. Wars between American Indians and the American military went on into the early twentieth century.

In 1877, Chief Joseph of the Nez Percé surrendered. He said:

> I am tired of fighting. . . . I want to have time to look for my children, and see how many of them I can find. Maybe I shall find them among the dead. Hear me, my chiefs! I am tired. My heart is sick and sad. From where the sun now stands I shall fight no more forever.[3]

Adventure and Easy Money

After the Civil War, some men (and a few women) were not looking for jobs at all. They were looking for adventure and easy money. They had spent years riding hard and fighting hard. They lived the same way when the war was over. Some became train robbers, bank robbers, cattle rustlers, and general Wild West troublemakers.

Several of the troublemakers had ridden with Confederate troops called Quantrill's Raiders. Before the war, William Quantrill was a schoolteacher, a gambler, and a wanted man for horse thievery and murder. During the war, he gained the title of the "bloodiest man in American history" before he was killed in an 1864 battle.[4]

Jesse James was fifteen when he began riding with Quantrill's Raiders. Jesse's brother Frank

Gold Rush Sesquicen-tennial

The *Sacramento Bee* newspaper has produced a Web site to commemorate the California Gold Rush days. Time lines, maps, photographs, and information on the routes to California are included.

Access this Web site from http://www.myreportlinks.com

was also a Raider. After the Civil War, the James brothers formed an outlaw gang. Former Raider Cole Younger and his three brothers soon joined them. The James Gang robbed banks, trains, stagecoaches, stores, and individuals. Jesse James killed a half dozen or more men.

Some people thought of Jesse James as a kind of Robin Hood. They claimed that he stole from the rich and gave to the poor—though there is no actual evidence of that.[5] The Youngers were killed or captured in 1876, and in 1882, a gang member named Bob Ford shot Jesse James in the back and claimed the ten thousand-dollar reward posted for him. Frank James gave himself up soon after his brother's murder, but was never convicted of any crime. He retired from the outlaw life.

People became determined to bring order to the Wild West. Some just wanted to protect the communities where they lived; some were out-siders hired for the job.

▶ Detectives on the Trail

In 1850, a Chicago deputy sheriff named Allan Pinkerton set up a private agency to catch train robbers. The agency motto was "We Never Sleep." Pinkerton's National Detective Agency became successful and famous. He hired the first American female detective, Kate Warne, and soon hired other women as detectives.[6]

▲ Famous outlaw Jesse James was killed when he was shot in the back by Bob Ford, a member of James's own gang. This image is of James laying in his coffin.

One of Pinkerton's best detectives, Charles Angelo Siringo, chased down the James Gang. Pinkerton agents were so good at protecting railroads that some outlaws stopped robbing trains. In 1908, when the United States government set up the Federal Bureau of Investigation, they used Pinkerton's National Detective Agency as a model.[7]

▶ The Bandit Queen

Myra Belle Shirley spent her life among outlaws and became one herself. Her older brother might have ridden with Quantrill's Raiders. After the war, the James and Younger brothers sometimes hid out at her family's Texas farm. Belle ran away with one outlaw and later married another, Sam Starr. She saw herself as a bandit queen, often dressed in velvet and feathers. She got the reputation of being the mastermind behind her own gang.

In 1883, Belle Starr was caught and convicted by Judge Isaac C. Parker, known as the "hanging judge." Belle Starr did her time in jail, but she was later accused of disguising herself as a man and taking part in a bank robbery.

Like several other outlaws, Belle Starr was shot in the back and killed. After her 1889 death, the *National Police Gazette* wrote a glamorous version of her life in *Belle Starr, the Bandit Queen, or The Female Jesse James.*

▲ The Younger Brothers, Robert and James, and their father, Cole, were members of the James Gang. This image is of the Younger family: Henrietta (top), Cole (far right), Robert (left) and James (bottom).

▶ Kids and Poets

The outlaws of the Wild West included a variety of gunslingers and thieves. One teenager who killed, stole, and fell in with gangs was called Billy the Kid. William H. Bonney, Jr., was said to have killed at least twenty-seven men before he reached the age of twenty-one. But that was as long as the Kid would live.

Lawman Pat Garrett captured Billy the Kid in 1880. The Kid was tried, convicted of murder, and sentenced to hang. But the Kid escaped from jail. Pat Garrett tracked down Billy the Kid again, and this time the lawman shot the outlaw.

Charles Boles was a completely different kind of outlaw. Boles was a polite, gentlemanly stage robber known as Black Bart. It was said that he never even loaded his gun. Black Bart wrote poetry and left it at the scenes of his crimes. Here is one example:

Here I lay me down to sleep

To wait the coming morrow

Perhaps success perhaps defeat

And everlasting Sorrow

Yet come what will, I'll try it once,

My condition can't be worse,

And if theres money in that box

'Tis munny in my purse.[8]

Allan Pinkerton (left), President Abraham Lincoln, and Major General John McClernand at Antietam, Maryland, during the Civil War. Pinkerton was a well-known detective.

The Wells Fargo company offered rewards and hired detectives to track down stage robbers. Two of their detectives finally caught up with Black Bart. After his four-year jail term, Bart declared that he was through with crime—as well as writing poetry.[9]

Lawmen and Outlaws

In the real Wild West, there was not always a clear difference between the good guys and the bad guys. The author O. Henry (real name William Sydney Porter) wrote that only one out of six outlaws had a "bad heart." "Five out of six Western outlaws are just cowboys out of a job and gone wrong. The sixth is a tough from the East who dresses up like a bad man and plays some low-down trick that gives the boys a bad name."[10]

On the other hand, some famous lawmen were also gamblers and heavy drinkers. Others crossed back and forth between enforcing the law and breaking it. Tom Horn, for example, worked as an army scout and a Pinkerton detective. Then he became a hired gun for cattlemen having problems with rustlers. He killed cattle thieves for pay—as much as five hundred dollars per man. Horn said, "Killing men is my specialty. I look at it as a business."[11] But perhaps Horn was too fond of killing. He was tried and found guilty of the murder of a fourteen-year-old boy, and hanged for the crime.

Wild Bill Hickok was a stagecoach driver, a scout for General Custer's cavalry, a sheriff or marshal in several western towns, a dime-novel hero, a performer in Buffalo Bill Cody's plays and Wild West shows, a professional gambler, and a famous gunfighter. He was said to have killed about a hundred men.

In 1871, Wild Bill was hired as marshal of Abilene, Kansas. Like most marshals, he was responsible for more than arresting outlaws. His tasks included keeping the town streets and sidewalks clean and litter free, doing paperwork,

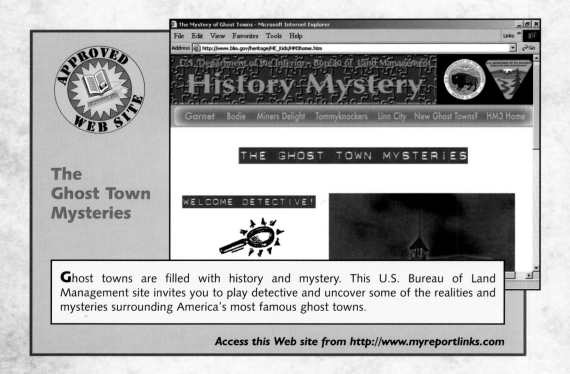

The Ghost Town Mysteries

Ghost towns are filled with history and mystery. This U.S. Bureau of Land Management site invites you to play detective and uncover some of the realities and mysteries surrounding America's most famous ghost towns.

Access this Web site from http://www.myreportlinks.com

rounding up stray cattle, and shooting unlicensed dogs. The citizens of Abilene finally decided that their town was still too rowdy, and fired Hickok from his job.

In 1875, Hickok became the marshal in Deadwood, South Dakota, one of the wildest of the mining towns. A gunman named Jack McCall killed the marshal, shooting him from behind while Hickok was playing poker. The hand Wild Bill Hickok was holding—black aces and black eights—is still called "the dead man's hand."

There were fifteen children in the Dalton family, and their mother tried hard to keep them on the right side of the law. She did not want them to go bad like her brother's kids, the Youngers. Several of the Dalton boys were United States government marshals.

But in spite of their mother's efforts, the Dalton marshals stole some horses. When they were forced out of their jobs, three of the Daltons formed an outlaw gang. In 1892, angry citizens gunned them down when they tried to rob two banks at once in Coffeyville, Kansas.

Holliday, Earp, and Masterson

Doc Holliday, a skillful gambler, was forced to flee Dallas, Texas, after shooting a local citizen. Holliday was involved in other gunfights and knife fights, and soon a reward was posted for him.

Holliday was once saved from death by Mary Catherine Elder, also known as "Big Nose Kate." When Holliday had been arrested and seemed likely to be hanged by vigilantes, Kate broke him out of jail.

Holliday became friends with lawman and gambler Wyatt Earp. In 1878, Earp was assistant marshal in Dodge City, Kansas. Doc Holliday joined the side of Wyatt Earp and his brother, Morgan Earp, for a famous gun battle. The Earps and Holliday killed several members of another gang—the Clantons—in the gunfight at the O.K. Corral.

Another of Wyatt Earp's friends was Bat Masterson, known to be a gambler and heavy drinker. Masterson was a sheriff or marshal in several western towns. In 1905, President Teddy Roosevelt appointed Bat Masterson a marshal in New York State.

When Masterson was later offered the marshal's job in the Oklahoma Territory, he turned it down. He said that he would just be inviting gun battles with men trying to make a reputation for themselves. Masterson resigned from the lawman business in 1907, and took a job as a sports editor.

▶ The Code of the West

There were certain ideas about how people should behave in the Wild West. It was an unwritten code,

Bat Masterson was a famous sheriff of the Old West. Masterson was a close friend of legendary marshal Wyatt Earp.

but those who violated it could find themselves without friends and with many enemies. A real cowboy was expected to be loyal to his or her friends, to feed and house travelers, to fight fairly, and to be honest. A handshake was considered as good as a written contract.

In general, people in the Wild West were expected to mind their own business. Men were supposed to treat women with respect. And many men believed that they must fight anyone who insulted or threatened them.

▶ Mark Twain

Mark Twain was a newspaper editor in Virginia City, Nevada, in the early 1860s. In his autobiography, Twain wrote:

> In those early days dueling suddenly became a fashion in the new territory of Nevada and by 1864 everybody was anxious to have a chance in the new sport, mainly for the reason that he was not able to thoroughly respect himself so long as he had not killed or crippled somebody in a duel or been killed or crippled in one himself.[12]

Twain added that he had no interest in dueling. Still, he got caught up in the craze. Urged on by eager buddies, Twain got into a hot argument with the owner of a rival newspaper. Finally, Twain gave in to his friends and challenged the other man, a Mr. Laird, to a duel.

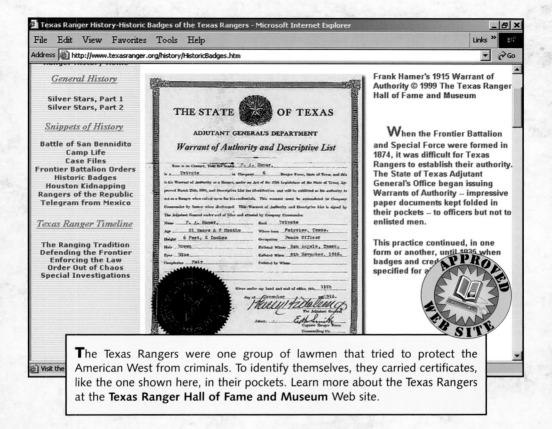

Frank Hamer's 1915 Warrant of Authority © 1999 The Texas Ranger Hall of Fame and Museum

When the Frontier Battalion and Special Force were formed in 1874, it was difficult for Texas Rangers to establish their authority. The State of Texas Adjutant General's Office began issuing Warrants of Authority -- impressive paper documents kept folded in their pockets -- to officers but not to enlisted men.

This practice continued, in one form or another, until 1935 when badges and cred[entials were] specified for a[ll.]

The Texas Rangers were one group of lawmen that tried to protect the American West from criminals. To identify themselves, they carried certificates, like the one shown here, in their pockets. Learn more about the Texas Rangers at the **Texas Ranger Hall of Fame and Museum** Web site.

Twain and a friend named Steve Gillis went out to practice shooting. They discovered that Twain could not even hit a barn door, much less a target. Knowing that Laird was nearby, Steve Gillis shot a small bird. They let Laird believe that Twain had made the difficult shot, and Laird withdrew from the duel.

Twain's life was saved. He wrote that, "if the duel had come off, he would have . . . filled my skin with bullet-holes."[13]

THE PLAYERS ON THE WILD WEST STAGE

Quite a variety of characters contributed to the Wild West. Here is a bit of information about some of them.

▷ Black Bart

His real name was Charles E. Boles, or Bolton. No one is certain of where Black Bart was born, but most believe he was born in 1829 in Norfolk County, England. When he was young, his parents moved to Jefferson County, New York. Then, he lived an apparently ordinary life in Illinois and California before becoming a stagecoach robber in 1875. He is believed to have held up twenty-eight stagecoaches before he was tracked down by Pinkerton agents in 1883. Black Bart was known for leaving bits of his original poetry at the scenes of his crimes. He served his four years in jail, then disappeared from sight. Some say he died in 1917, but others believed that he lived longer under a different identity.

▶ Jim Beckwourth, or James Pierson Beckwith

Beckwourth was a biracial man, born a slave in Virginia in 1798. His white father legally freed him in St. Louis in 1810. In 1823, Beckwourth signed on with a fur-trading expedition. He lived among the Crow American Indians for about six years, then became a guide for forty-niners rushing to California in search of gold. In 1856, he met journalist Thomas D. Bonner, who later wrote *The Life and Adventures of James P. Beckwourth, Mountaineer, Scout, Pioneer and Chief of the Crow Nation of Indians*. Beckwourth served as a guide and scout for the United States military, and died in 1866 during a visit back with the Crow people.

Grant-Kohrs Ranch National Historic Site

What was once one of the largest and best-known cattle range ranches in the country was turned into a living museum in 1972. The 1,500-acre park has ninety historic structures and is maintained as a national historic site. Learn more about the history of cattle ranching when you visit the site.

Access this Web site from http://www.myreportlinks.com

▶ Billy the Kid

The Kid was born William H. Bonney, Jr., in New York City in 1859. His original name might have been Henry McCarty, but when he became an outlaw he used William H. Bonney. When Billy was a child, his family moved to Kansas and then to New Mexico. He began hanging out in bars and killing at an early age. In 1881, he was killed while still in his early twenties by Sheriff Pat Garrett.

▶ Black Elk

Also known as Nicholas Black Elk, he was born an Oglala Sioux in Wyoming in 1863. He became an important Sioux religious leader and shamanic healer. Black Elk lived on the Pine Ridge

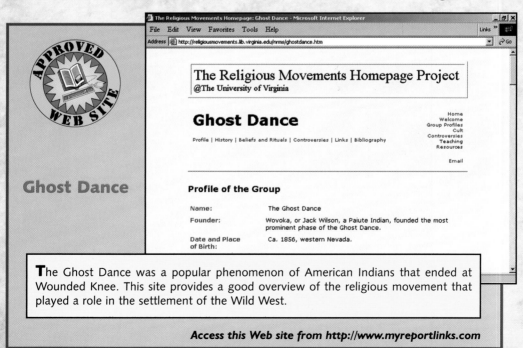

Ghost Dance

The Ghost Dance was a popular phenomenon of American Indians that ended at Wounded Knee. This site provides a good overview of the religious movement that played a role in the settlement of the Wild West.

Access this Web site from http://www.myreportlinks.com

Reservation in South Dakota, and he was there during the 1890 massacre at Wounded Knee. From 1886 to 1889, he traveled with Buffalo Bill's Wild West Show. Black Elk became an Episcopalian, and later converted to Catholicism. Black Elk met the poet John G. Neihardt, and they worked together on the influential 1932 book, *Black Elk Speaks*.[1] He passed away in 1950.

Daniel Boone

Daniel Boone was born in Pennsylvania in 1734 to a family of Quakers. When his family settled in North Carolina, Boone explored the Kentucky region. He helped to make a trail through the Cumberland Gap and to build the Wilderness Road into Kentucky. One of the first settlements in Kentucky was Boonesborough, where Boone moved with his wife and daughter in 1775. Boone was captured by Shawnee American Indians in 1778 and adopted as a

Daniel Boone was a congressman, explorer, and woodsman. He led the party that built the Wilderness Road into Kentucky, helping open the area to American settlement.

son by the chief. However, he escaped to warn settlers of a coming attack. Boone later moved on to the Louisiana Territory, still living as a hunter and trapper until his death in 1820.

Jim Bridger

He was born in Virginia in 1804. When his family moved to Illinois, Bridger began trapping furs along the Missouri River. For twenty years, Bridger traveled on foot around a huge area between the Canadian border, the Missouri River, the Colorado–New Mexico border, and Idaho and Utah. Bridger was always interested in exploring new territory. Landmarks named for him include Bridger Range (Montana), Bridger Peak (southern Wyoming), Bridger Pass (southern Wyoming), and the Bridger National Forest (western Wyoming). He died in 1881.

Ned Buntline

Author Ned Buntline's real name was Edward Zane Carroll Judson. Born in 1823, he was actually a New Yorker. In 1844, Buntline began writing stories for magazines. For a short time, he published his own *Ned Buntline's Magazine,* then *Ned Buntline's Own* newspaper. He was lynched for murder in Tennessee but was secretly cut down and released. Back in New York City, he spent time in jail for taking part in a riot. In the 1850s, Buntline helped organize the Know-Nothing political movement. During the Civil War, he joined the Union Army but was discharged for drunkenness. Buntline's more than four hundred sensational novels brought him financial success. In 1871, he also became a hymn writer and lecturer for the temperance movement, and he lived until 1886.

John Colter

John Colter was born in Virginia around 1775. In 1803, he joined the Lewis and Clark Expedition. In

John Colter explored the territory that became Yellowstone National Park. This is an image of Old Faithful, Yellowstone's well-known geyser.

1806, he became a trapper and guide in the West. Colter crossed the Teton Mountain Range on foot and traveled the area now included in Yellowstone National Park. He guided expeditions of trappers along the Missouri River and furnished valuable information for maps of western territory, before dying in 1813.

Kit Carson or Christopher Carson

Born in Kentucky in 1809, he soon moved with his family to Missouri. When his father died, young Kit was apprenticed to a saddle maker. In 1826, he ran away and traveled to Santa Fe and New Mexico. He made his home in Taos, New Mexico, and made his living as a wagon driver, cook, guide, and hunter. In 1842, Carson was hired as a guide by John C. Frémont for his western expeditions. Frémont highly praised Carson's skill and courage. In the West, Carson became a notable fighter against American Indians. At the end of the Civil War, he was made brigadier general in command of Fort Garland, Colorado. Carson passed away in 1868.

Davy Crockett or David Crockett

Crockett was born in Tennessee in 1786. In 1821 and again in 1823, he was elected to the Tennessee state legislature. In 1827, he was elected to the first of his three terms in the United States

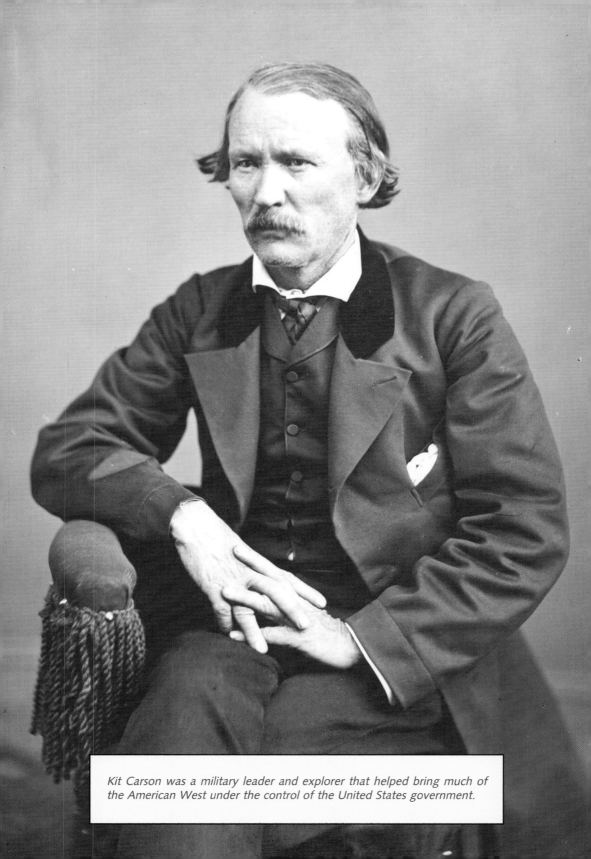

Kit Carson was a military leader and explorer that helped bring much of the American West under the control of the United States government.

House of Representatives. Crockett was well known for his backwoods humanity and manner and his sharp comments on politics. In 1835, Crockett left Tennessee for Texas, where he died in 1836 at the Battle of the Alamo.

Calamity Jane

Martha Jane Cannary was born around 1852 in Missouri. In 1865, she moved with her family to Montana. Calamity Jane grew up in rough mining towns, and she sometimes dressed as a man and boasted of being a Pony Express rider or a frontier scout. During an 1878 smallpox epidemic, she heroically nursed the ill. She became a western legend, partly because the Sioux Indians never harmed her because they knew that she was good with a rifle.[2] After Wild Bill Hickok died, Calamity Jane claimed that they had been married. She died in Deadwood in 1903 and was buried next to Hickok.

Buffalo Bill Cody

William Frederick "Buffalo Bill" Cody was born in Iowa in 1846. His family moved to Kansas, and in 1857, Cody's father died. Cody earned the family's living by working for supply trains and a freighting company. He tried out the California goldfields in 1859 and rode for the Pony Express in 1860. Cody worked as an army scout and a buffalo hunter—adventures that were written up and

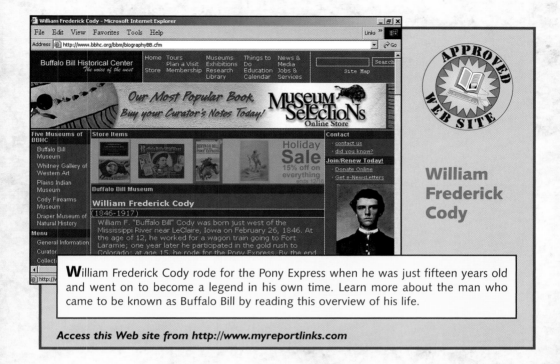

William Frederick Cody rode for the Pony Express when he was just fifteen years old and went on to become a legend in his own time. Learn more about the man who came to be known as Buffalo Bill by reading this overview of his life.

Access this Web site from http://www.myreportlinks.com

exaggerated in Ned Buntline's novels. After his stage appearances, Cody organized Buffalo Bill's Wild West Show, which toured successfully throughout the United States and Europe. He died in 1917.

▶ **Wyatt Earp**

Wyatt Earp was born in 1848 in Illinois. He became a gambler, gunfighter, and law officer in Wichita and Dodge City, Kansas, and a guard for Wells Fargo & Company in Tombstone, Arizona. In 1881, Wyatt Earp, his brothers Virgil and Morgan, and their friend, Doc Holliday, were involved in the O.K. Corral gunfight. In 1882, Wyatt Earp left

Tombstone. Earp operated saloons in California, Alaska, and Nevada. He settled in Los Angeles, California, where he was an advisor on several silent movie Westerns until he died in 1929.[3]

Mike Fink

No one knows for sure when Mike Fink was born or when he died. He is believed to have been born around 1770 in Pennsylvania. He was a keelboat-man on the flatboats of the Ohio and Mississippi rivers. In 1822, he became a trapper along the Missouri River. He was killed in a shoot-out near the mouth of the Yellowstone River sometime around 1823. Fink was noted as a marksman, fighter, and teller of tall tales. Because of the many stories about him, few details of Mike Fink's real life are known.

Geronimo

American Indian hero Geronimo was born in Arizona in 1829 and became an Apache leader. He led raids during

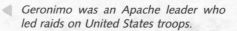

Geronimo was an Apache leader who led raids on United States troops.

the Indian Wars—struggles between American Indians and the United States military. Several times, Geronimo escaped capture. In 1886, he surrendered and was deported to Florida. He later settled down to farming in Oklahoma and adopted Christianity. He became a celebrity, appearing at the St. Louis World's Fair and in Theodore Roosevelt's inaugural procession. He died in 1909.

Doc Holliday

John Henry "Doc" Holliday was born in 1852 and raised in Georgia. In 1872, he graduated from the Pennsylvania College of Dental Surgery. Holliday moved west for his health and practiced dentistry in Dallas, Texas. Discovering that he had gambling skills, he began moving around the West. Holliday gained a reputation as a drinker, fighter, and gambler. He made friends with Wyatt Earp, and joined the Earps at the O.K. Corral gunfight in Tombstone, Arizona. He died of tuberculosis in Colorado in 1887.

Tom Horn

Born in Missouri in 1860, Tom Horn was beaten by his father, and left home at age thirteen. As a lawman and then a hired gun, Horn seemed to look on his own killings as an attempt to "beat out the bad" in the world.[4] He was said to have confessed to the murder for which he was hanged in 1903, but some historians believe that the confession was just a drunken boast.

Wild Bill Hickok

James Butler "Wild Bill" Hickok was born in Illinois in 1837. He called himself "William," after his father, and later was nicknamed "Wild Bill." He was tall and considered very handsome. Hickok worked as a Pony Express station attendant, wagon driver, army scout, guide, and gambler. In 1867, an article about Hickok in *Harper's Magazine* made him famous across the country. Afterward, he served as sheriff of Abilene, Kansas, and later worked as an entertainer alongside Buffalo Bill. He was killed—shot in the back—in Deadwood, South Dakota, in 1876.[5]

Chief Joseph

Chief Joseph of the Nez Perce (who call themselves Nimi'ipuu) Indians, was born in 1840 in Oregon. When his people were pressed to move to a reservation, Chief Joseph led them in an effort to escape to Canada. During his flight, he treated prisoners humanely and bought supplies from settlers rather than stealing them. He surrendered out of concern for the women, children, and elderly among his people. Chief Joseph's actions won respect among settlers of European descent. He ended his life on a reservation in Washington State, expiring in 1904.

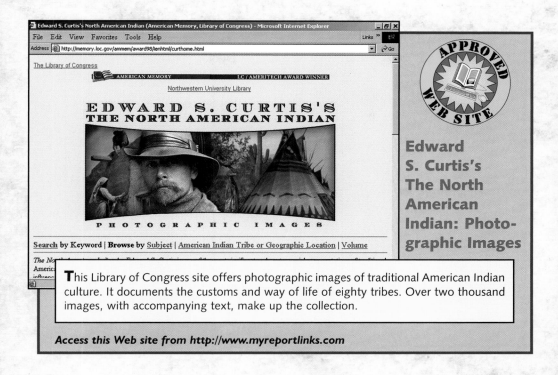

Edward S. Curtis's North American Indian (American Memory, Library of Congress) - Microsoft Internet Explorer

File   Edit   View   Favorites   Tools   Help   Links »

Address http://memory.loc.gov/ammem/award98/ienhtml/curthome.html   Go

The Library of Congress

AMERICAN MEMORY   LC / AMERITECH AWARD WINNER

Northwestern University Library

EDWARD S. CURTIS'S
THE NORTH AMERICAN INDIAN

PHOTOGRAPHIC IMAGES

Search by Keyword | Browse by Subject | American Indian Tribe or Geographic Location | Volume

Edward S. Curtis's The North American Indian: Photographic Images

This Library of Congress site offers photographic images of traditional American Indian culture. It documents the customs and way of life of eighty tribes. Over two thousand images, with accompanying text, make up the collection.

Access this Web site from http://www.myreportlinks.com

▶ Jesse James (1847–1882) and Frank James (1843–1915)

The James brothers were born in Missouri. After the Civil War, the James brothers led an outlaw gang that robbed banks, stagecoaches, stores, and individuals. Many people of Missouri believed that the James brothers were persecuted by lawmen because they had fought on the Confederate side during the war. The James Gang was broken up by lawmen in 1876, and they formed a new gang in 1879. Jesse was shot in the back and killed by one of his gang who wanted to collect the reward posted for him. Frank James later

▲ Frank James was the brother of outlaw Jesse James. Frank James was an outlaw himself, who decided to turn himself in after his brother was killed.

gave himself up, spent time in jail, and then retired to a quieter life in Missouri.

Bat Masterson

Bartholomew "Bat" Masterson was born in Canada in 1853 and grew up in Illinois and Kansas. He also used the name William Barclay Masterson. At nineteen, Masterson became a buffalo hunter and scout near Dodge City, Kansas. He was a sheriff, deputy United States marshal, saloon keeper, and gambler. Masterson also worked briefly with Wyatt Earp at Earp's saloon in Tombstone, Arizona. He moved to Denver, Colorado, but was asked to leave in 1902. Masterson then moved to New York City. President Theodore Roosevelt made him deputy United States Marshal for the southern district of New York. Masterson later wrote magazine features and became a sports editor for the *New York Morning Telegraph*. He died in 1921.

Annie Oakley

Her real name Phoebe Ann Moses, Annie Oakley was born in Ohio in 1860. As a child, she became a crack shot with a rifle. According to legends about her, little Annie hunted and sold game, and paid off the mortgage on the family farm. At age fifteen, Annie Oakley won a shooting match with marksman Frank E. Butler. They were married and

▲ Annie Oakley was a crack shot, that is, she had incredible aim with a gun. She showed off her talents as part of Buffalo Bill's Wild West Show.

toured together. In 1885, the couple joined Buffalo Bill's Wild West Show. She passed away in 1926.

Allan Pinkerton

Allan Pinkerton was born in Scotland in 1819 and died in 1884. When he was still a child, Allan's father died. The family was left in poverty, so Allan found work as a cooper (barrel maker). When he became involved in a movement for social reform, Pinkerton was threatened with arrest. In 1842, he fled to the United States. He worked as a cooper near Chicago. After he captured a gang of counterfeiters while on an island looking for material to make barrels, Pinkerton was appointed the county's deputy sheriff. That is when he decided to become a detective. He organized his own Pinkerton's National Detective Agency in 1850. After years of success, Pinkerton wrote several books about detecting and spying.

Butch Cassidy and the Sundance Kid

Cassidy's real name was Robert LeRoy Parker when he was born in Utah in 1866. He spent two years working as a cowboy. Then Cassidy teamed up with other outlaws, robbing trains and banks and stealing horses and cattle. When lawmen were closing in on them, Butch Cassidy and the Sundance Kid (Harry Longbaugh) escaped to

South America. Etta Place, a woman who went with them, returned. The two outlaws were surrounded and supposedly killed in Bolivia in 1909. Other stories have them surviving and returning quietly to the United States.

Belle Starr

Belle Starr, or Myra Belle Shirley, (1848–89) was born in Missouri. She moved with her family to Texas in 1872. After the Civil War, the family ranch became a meeting ground for the James brothers and the Younger brothers, all outlaws. As Belle Starr the Bandit Queen, she would be involved with outlaws for the rest of her life. She served three months in the Michigan federal penitentiary for stealing horses. In 1889, Belle Starr was shot in the back and killed at an Arkansas ranch. No one is sure why.

Sitting Bull

Tatanka Iyotanka, better known as Sitting Bull, was born in the Dakota Territory in 1831. Around 1867, he was made chief of the Lakota Sioux nation. When the buffalo herds on which they depended for food and clothing had been reduced to nearly nothing, many Sioux surrendered to the United States military. In 1877, Sitting Bull led his remaining followers to Canada, but famine forced him to return and surrender. In 1885, Sitting Bull

Sitting Bull was one of the leaders of the Sioux Nation. While being pursued by the U.S. Army, he led his followers to temporary safety in Canada. However, he was eventually captured. He was later killed while living on a reservation.

joined Buffalo Bill's Wild West show and became internationally famous. However, in 1889, the American Indian religious Ghost Dance movement aroused alarm among the military. In 1890, Indian police and soldiers were sent to arrest Sitting Bull, and the chief and his son, Crow Foot, were killed when his warriors tried to rescue him.

Jedediah Smith

Jedediah Smith (1798–1831) was born in New York State. While still a teenager, he traveled to the Rocky Mountains as part of a fur-trading team. He took a party through the important South Pass in 1824, located in what is now Wyoming. Smith ranged north to the Canadian border down across the entire Southwest. He opened up fur-trapping territory and discovered trails that pioneers would soon use. He was eventually killed near the Cimarron River by a group of Comanche Indians.

THE WILD WEST THEN AND NOW

Toward the end of the 1800s, the Wild West got tamer. Many of the ways that marked it as "wild" simply disappeared. For example, the last big cattle drive to Dodge City was completed in 1881. Some states passed laws actually forbidding cattle from other states to cross their territory. Farmers also fenced their fields with barbed wire. And so the West became a quieter land of farms, fences, towns, and cities. Even the days of western outlaws came to an end.

▷ The Last Legendary Outlaw Gang

In 1899, Robert Parker and his partner, Harry Longbaugh, led a gang of outlaws in bank and train robberies across the West. Best known as Butch Cassidy and the Sundance Kid, they called their gang The Wild Bunch. Many people considered Butch Cassidy a kind of Robin Hood (just as they had thought of Jesse James). Settlers and small ranchers believed that Cassidy was fighting on their side, against big cattle outfits that were taking over the West.

But by the end of the nineteenth century, it was hard to be an outlaw. There were more lawmen and fewer places to hide. The railroads hired Pinkerton agents to chase down the Wild Bunch. Realizing that the lawmen who were after them would never give up until they were caught or killed, Cassidy and Sundance left the country.

In 1901, the two outlaws and Etta Place fled to South America. They tried running an honest ranch in Argentina, but soon went back to robbing banks. Etta Place returned to the United States, and Bolivian Army troops caught up with Cassidy

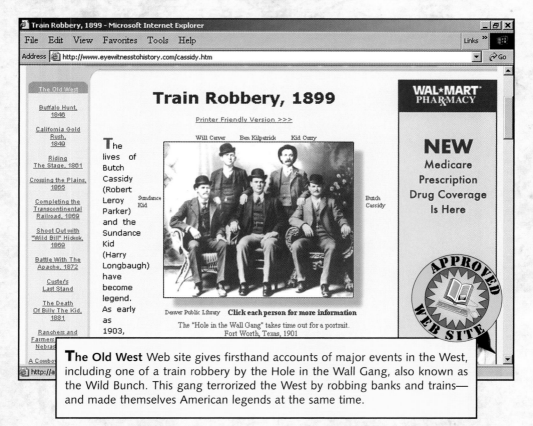

The Old West Web site gives firsthand accounts of major events in the West, including one of a train robbery by the Hole in the Wall Gang, also known as the Wild Bunch. This gang terrorized the West by robbing banks and trains—and made themselves American legends at the same time.

and Sundance in Bolivia. The outlaws were supposedly killed in 1909 in a final battle with the Bolivian military. But according to some stories, Butch Cassidy and the Sundance Kid survived the shootout.

In 1969, reporters talked with Butch Cassidy's sister, who was then eighty-six years old. She told them that Cassidy had visited her in 1925. She said that Cassidy had spent his last years as a trapper and prospector and had died in Spokane, Washington, in 1937. Some scholars claim that Butch Cassidy wrote an account of his life years after his supposed death.[1]

Whatever happened to them, Butch Cassidy and the Sundance Kid were legendary. In fact, the whole Wild West came to be more legend than reality.

Buffalo Bill Goes on With the Show

In the 1870s, Buffalo Bill Cody, Texas Jack, and Wild Bill Hickok played themselves on stage. Soon, Buffalo Bill decided to

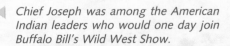

◄ *Chief Joseph was among the American Indian leaders who would one day join Buffalo Bill's Wild West Show.*

make his act larger than any stage would hold. In 1883, he organized a four-hour outdoor spectacle featuring hundreds of animals, cowboys, and American Indians.

Famous American Indian chiefs such as Sitting Bull, Chief Joseph, and Geronimo joined the show. The performers included sharpshooters, trick riders, and ropers. They staged reenacted battles, buffalo hunts, American Indian war dances, races, and an attack on a stagecoach.

▶ The Main Attraction

Annie Oakley, also called "Little Sure Shot," was a favorite act. At thirty paces, she could shoot a playing card held on its edge and hit dimes or cards tossed into the air. She was famous for shooting a cigarette from her husband's lips. When the show went to Europe, she performed the same trick with Crown Prince Wilhelm of Germany.

Buffalo Bill's Wild West Show was a hit. It played in New York's Madison Square Garden and also toured Europe. Some people even credit Cody with inventing the term "Wild West."

In 1883, Black Elk of the Oglala Sioux traveled to London to perform with Buffalo Bill's show. Black Elk met England's Queen Victoria. The queen is said to have seen the show three times. When the Wild West show left, Black Elk and several others missed the boat going back to the United States. Fortunately, they found work with another traveling show and got to visit Paris, France, and other European cities.

In 1894, Buffalo Bill and Annie Oakley were recorded on film at Thomas Edison's Kinematograph Studio in West Orange, New Jersey.[2] Since Cody came to the movies before they were a widespread form of entertainment, he never got to be a movie star. Even so, his appearances helped create the movie Western.

The 101 Ranch Show

In the nineteenth century, the 101 Ranch was a working cattle outfit. On the 110,000 acres near Oklahoma City, Colonel George W. Miller and his family raised and herded cattle. In the early twentieth century, the family staged roundups and buffalo chases for public entertainment. At the "101

The 101 Ranch was a popular place for people to go see Wild West shows. It is estimated that as many as sixty-five thousand people took in a show there at once.

Ranch Real Wild West and Great Far East Show" visitors watched cowboys ride bucking mustangs and demonstrate their roping skills. This is considered to be the first rodeo.

As many as sixty-five thousand people at a time came to see the 101's Wild West shows. Guests included President Theodore Roosevelt and the humorist Will Rogers. The Apache warrior Geronimo also put in an appearance, wearing a top hat and riding in a convertible.

In 1911, the Miller family loaned New York Motion Picture Company one hundred cowboys and cowgirls, seventy-five American Indians, along with covered wagons and livestock. Like Buffalo Bill, they helped Western movies get started.

The Wild West in Story, Sound, and Pictures

Starting in 1903 with *The Great Train Robbery*, cowboy movies became very, very popular with

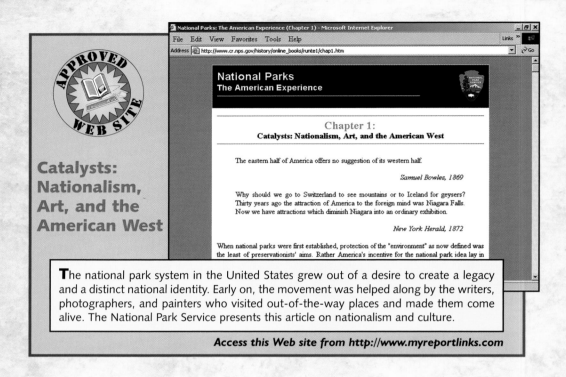

National Parks: The American Experience (Chapter 1) - Microsoft Internet Explorer

File   Edit   View   Favorites   Tools   Help   Links »

Address http://www.cr.nps.gov/history/online_books/runte1/chap1.htm   Go

National Parks
The American Experience

Chapter 1:
Catalysts: Nationalism, Art, and the American West

The eastern half of America offers no suggestion of its western half.

Samuel Bowles, 1869

Why should we go to Switzerland to see mountains or to Iceland for geysers?
Thirty years ago the attraction of America to the foreign mind was Niagara Falls.
Now we have attractions which diminish Niagara into an ordinary exhibition.

New York Herald, 1872

When national parks were first established, protection of the "environment" as now defined was
the least of preservationists' aims. Rather America's incentive for the national park idea lay in

**Catalysts:
Nationalism,
Art, and the
American West**

The national park system in the United States grew out of a desire to create a legacy and a distinct national identity. Early on, the movement was helped along by the writers, photographers, and painters who visited out-of-the-way places and made them come alive. The National Park Service presents this article on nationalism and culture.

Access this Web site from http://www.myreportlinks.com

Americans. Those Westerns—like other tall tales and legends—often had little to do with western reality. But sometimes the stories became entangled with reality in interesting ways.

In 1905, Tom Mix rode with the 101 Ranch performers in New York City's Madison Square Garden. He was billed as a cowboy and former marshal from Oklahoma, or perhaps from Mexico. Tom Mix was originally from Mix Run, Pennsylvania, and his only cowboying was done as a performer. Still, Mix looked the part, and he starred in about three hundred Wild West silent movies.

The real lawman, Wyatt Earp, spent his later years in Hollywood, as an advisor on Western movies. Tom Mix and Wyatt Earp became friends.[3] A 1985 movie about their friendship, *Sunset,* is perhaps no more fictional than most Wild West stories.

Owen Wister's 1902 novel *The Virginian* was the best seller of its time.[4] *The Virginian* was made into a movie at least five times. The most influential was probably the 1928 version starring Gary Cooper. In *The Virginian* and other movies, Cooper portrayed all the inner strength, honesty, and courage that cowboys were supposed to represent.

In 1907, O. Henry published a book of short stories called *Heart of the West*. He created a character called the Cisco Kid, based on legends about a Texas gambler and gunman. The Cisco Kid was featured in silent and sound movies, radio shows, and a 1950s television series.

▶ Portrayal of Western Heroes

By the 1950s, western heroes were noble, honest, decent, and brave. Hopalong Cassidy, Gene Autry, Roy Rogers, and Dale Evans would never strike a foul blow. Neither would the heroes of John Wayne's early movies. The 1948 movie *Red River* startled many viewers with its flawed heroes and its tough heroine. Even so, they all turned out to be good guys by the end.

THE
VIRGINIAN
BY
Owen Wister and Kirke La Shelle

△ The Virginian *was a hugely popular book by Owen Wister that glorified the cowboy lifestyle.*

In the radio and television series *Gunsmoke*, Matt Dillon was the marshal of Dodge City, Kansas. Marshal Dillon's character was based on Wyatt Earp, Bat Masterson, and other actual western lawmen.[5] On radio, Marshal Dillon often mentioned his friend Wild Bill Hickok.

The Westerns of the 1940s and 1950s told us how things were supposed to be. Cowboys did not break laws (unless the lawmen were villains). Bad behavior led to punishment. Good behavior usually led to happy endings.

Recent western stories have become more varied. Some seem more like mythology; others are realistic to the point of being gruesome. The heroes of Westerns live by their own code rather than by the rules of society.

But then, the Wild West was always as much fiction as reality.

▷ What Is Left of the Wild West Now?

Some Wild West towns have turned into modern towns. Last Chance Gulch became the main street of Helena, Montana. Today the Gulch is a pedestrian walking mall and shopping area.

Travelers also can visit the Wild West in places such as Abilene and Dodge City, Kansas; Virginia City, Nevada; Cimarron, New Mexico; Deadwood, South Dakota; and Cripple Creek, Colorado. Those towns have preserved their historic areas,

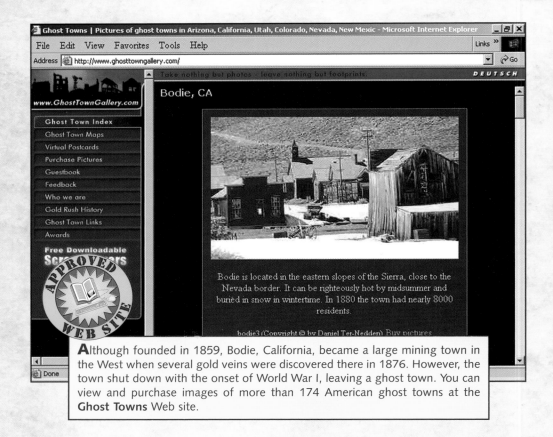

Ghost Towns | Pictures of ghost towns in Arizona, California, Utah, Colorado, Nevada, New Mexic - Microsoft Internet Explorer

File   Edit   View   Favorites   Tools   Help   Links »

Address http://www.ghosttowngallery.com/   Go

Take nothing but photos - leave nothing but footprints.   DEUTSCH

www.GhostTownGallery.com

Ghost Town Index

Ghost Town Maps
Virtual Postcards
Purchase Pictures
Guestbook
Feedback
Who we are
Gold Rush History
Ghost Town Links
Awards

Free Downloadable
Screensavers

Bodie, CA

Bodie is located in the eastern slopes of the Sierra, close to the Nevada border. It can be righteously hot by midsummer and buried in snow in wintertime. In 1880 the town had nearly 8000 residents.

bodie3 (Copyright © by Daniel Ter-Nedden) Buy pictures

Done

Although founded in 1859, Bodie, California, became a large mining town in the West when several gold veins were discovered there in 1876. However, the town shut down with the onset of World War I, leaving a ghost town. You can view and purchase images of more than 174 American ghost towns at the **Ghost Towns** Web site.

and they hold Wild West shows, rodeos, and other traditional events.

Thousands of other Wild West mining and farming towns were deserted. *Smithsonian Magazine* calls them "towns that lived fast and died young."[6] The remains of these ghost towns are scattered throughout the West. These are not re-creations, but the actual remains of old buildings and mines.

Some ghost towns offer museums, general stores, and places for visitors to stay. Others are privately owned and only sometimes open to the public.

Just as William F. Cody and the cowboys of Ranch 101 turned to producing entertainment, so do some cowboys today. In the late 1800s and early 1900s, ranchers started providing vacations for those who wanted to get out of cities and experience the West. Today, hundreds of dude ranches offer a bit of the Wild West for those who want to try it out. Some of these are even working cattle operations, where an easterner can become a "real" cowboy for a while.

Most of all, the Wild West is still with us in our stories. Even the heroes of spy and detective thrillers or science fiction tales are cowboys in different costumes. And those stories echo the message of Westerns—that a hero must be loyal to friends, dependable, self-reliant, brave, smart enough to outthink the villains, and skillful enough to stay alive. In those ways, tales of the Wild West apply to all our daily lives.

Report Links

The Internet sites described below can be accessed at http://www.myreportlinks.com

▶**New Perspectives on the West**
Editor's Choice On this Web site, take a look at the history of western expansion.

▶**Exploration of the West**
Editor's Choice Explore the Old West through photographs.

▶**The Pony Express National Museum**
Editor's Choice Access information about the Pony Express from this site.

▶**Transcontinental Railroad**
Editor's Choice Learn about the construction of the Transcontinental Railroad.

▶**The Gold Rush**
Editor's Choice This PBS guide to the California Gold Rush is a comprehensive source.

▶**Old West Legends: Adventures in the American West**
Editor's Choice This web portal has extensive information related to the American West.

▶**American Memory Timeline**
Learn more about American history through primary documents.

▶**America's Library**
Have fun learning about history when you visit this site.

▶**Catalysts: Nationalism, Art, and the American West**
Read the history behind the parks of the Wild West on this NPS Web site.

▶**Cowboy Facts and Legends**
This is a good starting place for discovering the men and women who helped settle the Wild West.

▶**Early California History: An Overview**
A good overview of early California history.

▶**Edward S. Curtis's The North American Indian: Photographic Images**
Explore the life and times of North American Indians through photographs.

▶**Ghost Dance**
This site has information about ghost dancing.

▶**The Ghost Town Mysteries**
This site will help you find out more about ghost town history.

▶**Ghost Towns**
Comprehensive information and resources about ghost towns are available here.

Report Links

The Internet sites described below can be accessed at
http://www.myreportlinks.com

▶ **Ghost Towns by Night Light**
To view ghost town buildings, visit this Web site.

▶ **Gold Rush Sesquicentennial**
This site celebrates 150 years of gold mining in California.

▶ **Golden Spike National Historic Site**
This is the National Park Service Web site for the Golden Spike National Historic Park.

▶ **Grant-Kohrs Ranch National Historic Site**
A National Park Service Web site with information about nineteenth-century range ranches.

▶ **History of the American West, 1860–1920**
To learn more about the settlement of the American West, visit this government site.

▶ **Homestead National Monument of America**
For information on homesteading, visit this National Park Service Web site.

▶ **John James Audubon**
The life of "The Birds of America" artist is summarized on this site.

▶ **Literature, Culture, Art, Photos of the Old West**
This is a list of resources containing images, articles, and other papers.

▶ **The Mountain Men**
This is a links page for information on the history of mountain men.

▶ **The Mountain Men: Pathfinders of the West 1810–1860**
This site has extensive information about mountain men and the fur trade.

▶ **The Old West**
Read firsthand accounts and overviews of historical moments in American history.

▶ **Pony Express National Historic Trail**
Learn about the Pony Express routes and trails on this site.

▶ **Texas Ranger Hall of Fame and Museum**
This site provides extensive information about the Texas Rangers law officers.

▶ **Wild Bill Hickok**
You can read a biography of Wild Bill Hickok on this site.

▶ **William Frederick Cody**
The life and times of Buffalo Bill Cody are covered on this site.

Army Corps of Engineers—A branch of the U.S. Army that is responsible for civilian projects such as building bridges or mapping out terrain.

canvas—A painting created on a tightly woven cotton cloth-covered frame. Also the name of the cloth itself.

cave (verb)—To cause something to collapse.

dime novels—Storybooks that usually contained exciting but greatly exaggerated stories of famous people of the Wild West.

engraving—An image carved into a wood block that was used for printing.

exaggerated—Made to seem more important, better, or worse than it really is.

expedition—Group trip made for a specific purpose, such as exploring.

fantastic—Fanciful, unrealistic, extreme.

footlights—A row of lights that is positioned across the floor, in the front of the stage.

frontier—Area on the edge of civilization being opened up by hunters and pioneers.

geyser—A hot spring that periodically shoots jets of water into the air.

keelboatman—Man who rows, tows, or poles a keelboat (a riverboat that has a keel).

mesa—Flat raised area with steep sides.

pelt—Skin of an animal with the fur still attached.

prospector—Person who explores an area searching for gold or other valuable minerals.

showman—Someone who puts on, or performs in, a play or stage show.

six-cent weeklies—Weekly newspapers that used to cost six cents, and often contained stories and images of the West.

steam drill—A steam-powered tool used for drilling holes in rock to clear the way to lay railroad track.

tabloid—Small-sized newspaper, usually with many pictures and sensational stories.

tan—To make an animal hide into leather by treating it with tannin (from tree bark).

vigilante—Citizen acting as an unofficial lawman.

Chapter 1. Telling the Stories

1. *Chicago Inter Ocean Magazine,* October 15, 1911, quoted in Joseph. G. Rosa, *Wild Bill Hickok: The Man and His Myth* (Lawrence: University Press of Kansas, 1996), pp. 175–176.

2. Mark Twain's Letters from Washington, Number IX, *Territorial Enterprise,* March 7, 1868, <http://www.twainquotes.com/teindex.html> (September 29, 2005).

3. "Mike Fink," *Moscow State University,* n.d., <http://crydee.sai.msu.ru/ftproot/pub/rec/music/lyrics/cs-uwp/folk/m/mike_fink> (November 11, 2005).

4. "Dime Novels and Penny Dreadfuls," *Stanford University Libraries/Academic Text Service,* n.d., <http://garamond.stanford.edu:9001/dp/owa/pnpack.draw?pid=597> (September 29, 2005).

5. John A. Dinan, "Cheap Thrills," *American Collector,* October 1975, excerpted in *The Texas Jack Scout,* Vol. XV, No. 3, August 2000, p. 15.

6. Frederick Hayes, "Buntline Hated the West," *Real West,* March 1960, vol. 3, no. 10, reprinted on *The Texas Jack Scout,* <www.texasjack.org/history.html#DIME NOVEL HERO> (September 29, 2005).

7. John A. Dinan, "Cheap Thrills," *American Collector,* October 1975, excerpted in *The Texas Jack Scout,* Vol. XV, No. 3, August 2000, p. 15.

8. William S.E. Coleman, "Buffalo Bill on Stage," *Players: The Magazine of American Theatre,* December–January, 1972, Vol. 47, No. 2, p. 80.

9. Larry McMurtry, "Inventing the West," *The New York Review of Books,* Vol. 47, No. 13, August 10, 2000.

10. Coleman, p. 81.

11. Louisa Frederici Cody with Courtney Riley Cooper, *Memories of Buffalo Bill* (New York: D. Appleton & Co., 1919), quoted in Coleman, p. 86.

12. Ibid.

Chapter 2. From Wilderness to Wild West

1. "Stephen A. Long," *nebraskastudies.org*, n.d., <http://www.nebraskastudies.org/0400/frameset_reset.html?http://www.nebraskastudies.org/0400/stories/0401_0111.html> (September 29, 2005).

2. "History of the North American Fur Trade," *thefurtrapper.com*, September 25, 2005, <http://www.thefurtrapper.com/rendezvous.htm> (September 29, 2005).

3. James Beckwourth, *The Life and Adventures of James Beckwourth, Mountaineer, Scout, Pioneer and Chief of the Crow Nation of Indians.* Written from his own dictation by T.D. Bonner (London, 1892), pp. 424–426.

4. Michael Trinklein, "Discoverers and Explorers: Who Really Found the Oregon Trail?" *The Oregon Trail*, 2003, <http://www.isu.edu/~trinmich/Discoverers.html> (September 29, 2005).

5. Ibid.

6. Michael Johnson, *The Real West* (London: Octopus Books, Ltd., 1983), p. 20.

7. Emily Zimmerman, "The Stuff of Legends: The Ways of the Mountain Men," *The Mountain Men: Pathfinders of the West 1810–1860*, n.d., <http://xroads.virginia.edu/~HYPER/HNS/Mtmen/lifestyle.html> (November 11, 2005).

8. Kit Carson, quoted in Larry McMurtry, "Inventing the West," *The New York Review of Books*, Vol. 47, No. 13, August 10, 2000.

9. Henry David Thoreau, "Walking," *The Atlantic Monthly*, June 1862.

Chapter 3. Legends, Land, and Gold

1. "The Oregon Trail," *AmericanWest.com*, 2005, <http://www.americanwest.com/trails/pages/oretrail.htm> (September 29, 2005).

2. Michael Trinklein, "Introduction," *The Oregon Trail*, 2003, <http://www.isu.edu/%7Etrinmich/Introduction.html> (September 29, 2005).

3. Merrill Mattes, *The Great Platte River Road*, pp. 85 &

82, quoted by Dr. Robert L. Munkres in "Trail Facts," *Oregon-California Trails Association,* 1996–2002, <http://www.octa-trails.org/TheLearningCenter/TrailFacts/default.asp> (September 29, 2005).

4. Michael Johnson, *The Real West* (London: Octopus Books, Ltd., 1983), p. 36.

5. Ibid., p. 40.

6. "Charlotte Parkhurst," *California State Historical Society,* 2000, <http://www.californiahistory.net/7_pages/early_pink.htm> (September 29, 2005).

7. Leonard Kubiak, "History of the Stagecoach in the West," *Fort Tumbleweed,* 1996–2005, <http://www.forttumbleweed.com/wellsfargo.html> (September 29, 2005).

8. Johnson, p. 55.

9. "Frequently Asked Questions," *The Pony Express Home Station,* September 22, 2005, <http://xphomestation.com/frm-faq.html> (September 29, 2005).

Chapter 4. Cowboys, Cowgirls, Outlaws, and Lawmen

1. Dee Brown, ed., et al, *The Wild West* (New York: Warner Books, 1993), p. 107.

2. Ibid., p. 108.

3. Chief Joseph, as reprinted at "Chief Joseph," *Spirit Voices,* 1997, <http://thegoldweb.com/voices/chiefjoseph.html> (September 30, 2005).

4. James D. Horan and Paul Sann, *Pictorial History of the Wild West* (New York: Crown, 1954), p. 26.

5. Ibid., p. 27.

6. "A Tradition is Born," *Court TV's Crime Library,* 2005, <http://www.crimelibrary.com/gangsters_outlaws/cops_others/pinkerton/2.html?sect=18> (September 29, 2005).

7. Brown, et al., pp. 142–143.

8. Horan and Sann, p. 83.

9. "The Story of Charles E. Boles aka Black Bart," *Shadows of the Past,* 1984–2005, <http://www.sptddog.com/sotp/bbpo8.html> (September 29, 2005).

10. O. Henry, "Holding Up a Train," as reposted by *Art Branch, Inc.,* n.d., <http://www.literaturecollection.com/a/o_henry/158/> (September 29, 2005).

11. Candy Moulton, *The Writer's Guide to Everyday Life in the Wild West* (Cincinnati, Ohio: Writer's Digest Books, 1999), p. 277.

12. Mark Twain, "Chapters from My Autobiography," 1906, as reposted by *Under the Sun,* 2005, <http://www.underthesun.cc/Classics/Twain/autobiography/autobiography8.html> (September 29, 2005).

13. Ibid.

Chapter 5. The Players on the Wild West Stage

1. Annenberg Media, "Native Voices: Authors: Black Elk (1863–1950) and John G. Neihardt (1881–1973)," *American Passages: A Literary Survey,* 1997–2005, <http://www.learner.org/amerpass/unit01/authors-5.html> (September 29, 2005).

2. Jone Johnson Lewis, "Calamity Jane," *Women's History,* 2005, <http://womenshistory.about.com/od/westernamerica/p/calamity_jane.htm> (September 29, 2005).

3. Chip Carlson, "Wyatt Earp," *Legends of America,* January 2004, <http://www.legendsofamerica.com/WE-WyattEarp6.html> (September 29, 2005).

4. "Tom Horn: Misunderstood Misfit," *The HistoryNet.com,* 2005, <http://www.thehistorynet.com/we/blgunfightermostmisunderstood/> (September 29, 2005).

5. David Wallechinsky and Irving Wallace, "Cowboy Biography James Wild Bill Hickok," *Gunslingers: Good Guys and Bad Guys of the Wild West,* 1975–1981, <http://www.trivia-library.com/b/cowboy-biography-james-wild-bill-hickock.htm> (September 29, 2005).

Chapter 6. The Wild West Then and Now

1. "History of Butch Cassidy, LeRoy Parker," *Utah!,* 2005, <http://www.utah.com/oldwest/butch_cassidy.htm> (September 29, 2005).

2. Michael Wallis, *The Real Wild West: The 101 Ranch and the Creation of the American West* (New York: St. Martin's Press, 1999), p. 395.

3. Dan Rice, "Tom Mix," *Wyatt Earp,* October 12, 2001, <http://www.gv.net/~syd/WyattSEarp/tommix.html> (September 29, 2005).

4. Wallis, pp. 211–212.

5. "Dodge City, Kansas," *AmericanWest.com,* 2005, <http://www.americanwest.com/pages/dodge.htm> (September 29, 2005).

6. "Wandering the Towns That Lived Fast and Died Young," *Smithsonian Journeys,* May 2001, <http://www .smithsonianmag.si.edu/journeys/01/may01/travel_tips .html> (September 29, 2005).

Bial, Raymond. *Ghost Towns of the American West.* Boston: Houghton Mifflin, 2001.

Freedman, Russell. *In the Days of the Vaqueros: America's First True Cowboys.* New York: Clarion Books, 2001.

Krohn, Katherine. *Women of the Wild West.* Minneapolis, Minn.: Lerner Publications, Co., 2000.

Langley, Andrew. *100 Things You Should Know About the Wild West.* Broomall, Pa.: Mason Crest, 2003.

Macy, Sue. *Bulls-Eye: A Photobiography of Annie Oakley.* Washington, D.C.: National Geographic Society, 2001.

Penderast, Tom and Sara. *Westward Expansion: Almanac.* Vol. I to III. Detroit, Mich.: U X L, 2000.

Rosa, Joseph G., *Wild Bill Hickok: Sharpshooter and U.S. Marshal of the Wild West.* New York: PowerPlus Books, 2004.

Savage, Candace. *Born to be a Cowgirl: A Spirited Ride Through the Old West.* Berkeley, Calif.: Tricycle Press, 2001.

Swanson, Wayne. *Why the West was Wild.* Ontario, Canada: Firefly Books, 2004.

Uschan, Michael V. *Westward Expansion.* San Diego, Calif.: Lucent Books, 2001.

Wadsworth, Ginger. *Words West: Voices of Young Pioneers.* New York: Clarion Books, 2003.